A Few Laughs, Right God?

Nancy Drummond

A FEW LAUGHS, RIGHT GOD? by Nancy Drummond

Published by:
Insight Publishing Group
8801 South Yale, Suite 410
Tulsa, OK 74137
918-493-1718

International Standard Book Number: 1-930027-03-6
Library of Congress Card Catalog Number: 99-97662

Dedicated to all those people who said:
"Be Quiet"
and
"Write it Down"

Well, here it is. I hope you enjoy reading it as much as I
enjoyed writing it.

To Joan + Bernie --
"Have a "few laughs"
with me and God -
Nancy Drummond

I would like to say thank you to:

my husband, Speight—who showed me his love and patience throughout this endeavor.

all my children—Carol, Barbara, Mary Lou, Nancy, Chris, Richard and Sarah.

my grandchild, Martha—who spent endless hours patiently listening to all my stories time and time again and gave me lots of input and support throughout these past months.

Last but not least my grandchild—Lisa, and my friends—Elaine, Jesse and Phil.

A special thanks to you, Lord, for without Your love and guidance none of this would have been possible.

A Few Laughs, Right God?

While driving from New Hampshire to Connecticut one hot sunny August afternoon, I was aware that my German Shepherd, Winnie, was in the backseat of my non-air-conditioned car suffering mightily from the heat. I stopped at a McDonald's for a giant cup of ice water, but Winnie refused to drink.

Three hours later, her panting now in high gear, I again offered her some relief but she simply stuck her long nose into the container splashing cold water all over me, still preferring to be her obstinate self. This time I was really annoyed with the animal and flung the remaining half-cup of water out the car window. Could there possibly be someone directly behind me on this busy highway? Absolutely; my rearview mirror told me so. As I watched an irate gentleman waving his finger as he pulled up beside me (Like owner, like dog—neither very tuned in).

Just before all this all took place, I had been talking to God about what purpose I served in His garden. St. Therese the little flower, says in her autobiography that we are all flowers in God's garden and we each have a definite purpose. The answer to my question, which I had received maybe twenty minutes prior to my thoughtless action, was: "A Few Laughs!"

One Sunday morning while driving to church, I became aware of God's sense of humor and how ridiculous He found some of our actions. For a period of time, I would laugh at what someone was relating to me or at what they were doing. I perceived God found those things very funny. "What are you laughing at?" would more than likely be their retort since no one else seemed to be aware of any humor in the situation. "God finds that very funny," I would reply. Needless to say, they found me to be very bizarre, more so than usual.

After three months of this "enlightenment" I attended my first healing mass with some ladies from my prayer group (I had previously observed people being prayed over at Father D'Orio's church in Massachusetts, but was not an active participant). It was an unsettling experience for me to have my friend, Andy, resting in the spirit at my feet and I had to have terror written all over my face as I stepped up for my turn. Father simply gazed at me for a few moments and then out of his mouth came "Boy, you really crack God up!" I knew you had a sense of humor, Lord!

Don't Do It

It was 1:30 A.M. Easter morning in West Palm Beach, Florida, where my husband happened to be stationed. Nancy, our three-year-old, awakened feeling ill with a high temperature. Since she had consumed as unknown amount of baby aspirin the previous evening and had to have her stomach pumped, we were told to watch closely for any sign of acid poisoning. At this time of night the Base infirmary was closed. The only alternative was to take her to the emergency room at North Palm Beach Hospital. My husband stayed home with the other children while I, a very stressed lady from all the previous evening's excitement, took off for the far end of the town.

Greeting us as we entered the dimly lit corridor of the emergency room were several dead bodies covered with sheets. No attendants were visible—no customers either. The only sound to be heard was coming from a male voice in a nearby room screaming, "Oh Lord, I know I have died and gone to hell!" He kept repeating, totally terrified.

Eventually, the doctor emerged from the patient's cubicle. The expression on my face must have been priceless as I gazed dumbfounded upon this creature with dark auburn hair, capped to his head like a helmet, a red goatee, stark white skin covering a gaunt face and black horn-rimmed glasses. All that was lacking was the pitchfork and the tail.

The poor soul, who was still yelling when I left, firmly believed that he had died and gone to hell. Today, I would have made some gesture toward assuring him this was not the case.

Back then I was too timid—not courageous enough. By the way, Nancy was fine. She had a slight ear infection.

Never have I seen another human being that looked like the doctor we encountered that Easter morning. Could this have been God's early Easter gift to you, patient? I was greatly impressed; hopefully, he was too—No More Booze!

The Sad Get Sadder and the Funny Get Funnier

Nursing homes are places where most people feel completely free to be themselves, to say whatever comes into there heads or to act in any manner they choose for the moment. I had often wondered who were nuttier, the ones inside or the ones outside.

My mom was placed in a nursing facility because my stepfather could no longer take care of her and we had moved many states away. At the time they called her deterioration hardening of the arteries, but today it would be referred to as Alzheimer's.

While visiting mother one afternoon, my friend and I were strolling up the hall with her when a lady approached us extremely angry with her son. He was an an officer who had been transferred overseas and had decided that this was where his mom belonged. She went on to explain that her husband was dead, whereupon my mom exclaimed, "That's the best kind to have!" The poor lady wasn't sure she had heard my mom's remark correctly so she repeated that her husband was dead. Mother gleefully replied once more, "That's the best kind to have!" My friend and I were trying with all our might to control our laughter. Who knows why my stepdad was on my mom's hit list, but he obviously was.

God, did you explode into laughter?

Waiting in the gathering room for my mom to appear one day, I watched a most interesting incident take place. An obviously troubled lady came in cuddling her doll in her arms. Rocking the baby, she chatted and sang to it. From the expression on her face, she was not a happy woman, but an extremely sad one. Another lady appeared who was quite attracted to this scene. Happy, happy was she—she even did a little dance while she stood there.

"What's the baby's name?" she asked, but received no response. The other poor soul simply kept rocking and singing, seemingly oblivious to her surroundings.

Finally, after repeating her inquiry as to the baby's name numerous times, she twittered and came forth with, "I know what that baby's name is. It's Hadda. It Hadda come!" And with that, she laughingly went on her way.

Too much God! Did you laughingly go on your way?

Money Matters

Somehow, I ended up with the job of treasurer for the local Church-School Association for a year. For twenty-five years of my married life, I was responsible for paying the bills in our family. I even remember cutting up my MasterCard because I could not bear to face those finance charges every month, but now my husband had assumed the financial affairs role. After relinquishing this duty at home, it was difficult for me to understand why I said "yes" to the church-school position. After all, math was never my favorite subject even though it was not a problem when I was in school. However, balancing a checkbook has always been my cross. So, when I announced to Monsignor that as a special Christmas gift for him and the Association I was going to balance their checkbook, he looked at me as if he hadn't heard me correctly—no comment forthcoming. I was not kidding!

By the way, at the end of the year they were only a few pennies short—a big improvement from when it was presented to me with several hundred dollars unaccountable. My husband sure does a great job balancing a checkbook! Thank you, Lord.

To Be or Not to Be

Saturday night, Monsignor from the local church, two couples, and my husband and I gathered for an evening of stimulating "social conversation" and "philosophical discussion." After the preliminary round of discussion, drinks, and chit-chat, I proceeded to the kitchen for the final preparation of our meal. Upon opening the oven door to check the roast, I could not believe my eyes. There sat a perfectly uncooked piece of meat. Apparently, I had never turned on the oven. Needless to say, we had plenty of time for "stimulating" conversation that evening!

Dinner was served around midnight. As we all animatedly spoke our piece during the meal, particularly the super-charged, over-tired ladies, Monsignor suddenly stopped eating, cleared his throat, and proclaimed to the world, "Whew, am I glad I'm celibate!"

Did you share this exaltation of celibacy too, Lord?

Asking Is Receiving—
Ready or Not

Upon entering 8:30 mass one morning, it occurred to me to ask God for perfect humility that day. The morning readings were in progress when I suddenly became aware that my shirt was not buttoned. Three unbuttoned spaces across my chest puckered up presenting a gaping hole for the whole world to see. Never mind the whole world, Father was seated facing me only about eight feet away (morning mass was usually conducted in a small chapel, not the main church.) All I could do was laugh at God's sense of humor—and so early in the morning too. There was a time when I would have died of embarrassment during this incident, but there is certainly one benefit of old age—you just don't seem to care much anymore. The embarrassing part was that I had to reach down and button my blouse right in front of Father's face.

When I approached him later to ask if he were aware of the early morning show, he said "No." God saved the priest and certainly gave me a lesson in humility. Ha! Ha!

Never Let the Right Foot Know What the Left Foot Is Doing

It was Christmas Eve and we were invited to our daughter's annual gathering of the clan. She asked us to please come early so that we could help her with the preparations.

Before the arrival of the guests, we all hurried to dress for the evenings festivities. I could not believe that I had brought two different shoes, very dissimilar brown pumps. How would I solve this dilemma? My dirty tennis shoes would not do and my daughter's feet were too small for me to borrow a pair of her shoes. I even attempted to ask if her husband had anything appropriate for me to wear (his feet were more my size). He did not. The odd shoes were conspicuous, but there wasn't much of an alternative. Hopefully, the crowd would be a big one so my mismatch wouldn't be noticed. It was a great party. No one seemed aware of my rather unusual foot attire.

Several weeks later my daughter and hostess of the Christmas Eve party, Mary Lou, mentioned to me that her husband, Dave, had seen his sister's friend in town that day. The friend mentioned to Dave that there was a very strange happening at his Christmas Eve party. He stated that while engaged in a deep philosophical conversation with his mother-in-law, he happened to look down at her feet. Oh well, scratch that conversation—no validity. Needless to say, any words of wisdom spoken that night were null and void.

My husband tells people that I should come to parties with a warning label. Too bad it wasn't there that night.

Beware of Middle-Aged Ladies

My daughter-in-law's mother and I used to play paddle tennis together back in the 70's at a private court in our small town. We became aware that the local Y was sponsoring a lady's paddle tennis tournament and decided, what do we have to lose?

Flight B seemed the appropriate division in which we could comfortably compete—we were not the best and certainly not the worst. Here were two middle-aged ladies, a bit overweight to say the least, not in the greatest physical shape taking on mostly thirty-year-olds who definitely had all the credentials for winning paddle tennis tournaments, including the desire. Well, what do you know? We won and were the talk of the town —or at least that's what I was told

God strikes again—this time with a paddle tennis racquet.

Are You a Nun?

My friend, Andy, came running in the bookstore at the shopping center to tell me that I should come outside immediately because there was a young gentleman in the parking area who accidentally ran into my truck and was beside himself with anxiety. As we approached the vehicle he came up to me. The first thing out of his mouth was "Are you a nun?"

"No, I'm not a nun."

He was extremely upset because it was his aunt's car, which he had borrowed for the afternoon. The damage to my truck was practically nil, but I got the usual insurance information from him and stated very clearly that I would pass it on to my husband.

Again, he came forth with, "Are you a nun?"

We chatted for bit while I tried to instill some peace in this poor agitated soul. During this encounter, Andy is doing everything possible to keep from laughing. As we parted company, his final shot was, "Are you sure you're not a nun?"

Pretty funny, Lord.

Who Needs to Eat?

An addiction to junk, not the edible kind, at a certain period of my life afforded God many opportunities to be amused.

It was Saturday and time for me to shop at the local Air Force Base Commissary. I only went once every two weeks, which meant there were many bags of groceries for a family of eight. After completing my shopping, I decided it might be a great idea to dash over to the local junk shop in Virginia before returning home. My husband was babysitting and hopefully, wouldn't be too upset with the thought of a few extra hours of "fun" with the kids.

Upon returning to the car after my junking expedition, I was shocked to find that all of my groceries were gone! How can one report this sort of thing to the police? As I drove toward home trying to figure out just how I was going to explain this fiasco to my husband, I suddenly remembered I never picked up those groceries!

When I appeared back at the commissary and located the young man who had been left waiting patiently with my groceries, all he could say was "Lady, what happened to you?" It was a little embarrassing having to explain that one both there and at home.

A Jokester
in Our Midst

Mary Lou, one of the twins in our family, had a very forthright approach to life; she tended to see the "tree for the forest." When the twins were two-and-a-half-years old, they were having a lively discussion in bed one evening before closing their eyes and going to sleep. Barbara, her twin sister, remarked that their friend next door had bitten her that day. Mary Lou's reply to that was, "Wow! She must have been hungry!"

❀❀❀❀

Mary Lou expressed great disappointment when I returned from the hospital with a new baby brother. I could not figure out why she was so visibly disturbed. She finally confided to me later that she was expecting kittens, maybe even a hundred by the size of my tummy. The only pregnancies that she had witnessed at the age of three were the mother cats in our alley that reproduced regularly. Mary Lou, at that time in her life, had a great love affair with soft, cuddly, baby kittens.

❀❀❀❀

When we moved to Maryland, we bought a house with a large open, tiled basement that provided a great space in which our five kids could play, particularly in cold or inclement weather. One day I was busy complaining about the big mess downstairs, since all the neighborhood children gathered there also and no one was very receptive to picking up at the end of fun time. Mary Lou remarked to me, "What you need mom, is a house without a basement."

My husband, Speight, decided to take all the kids to the local department store to purchase a birthday present for mom. Their unanimous decision was that I needed underwear more than anything else. When the clerk came to wait on them Mary Lou blurted out, "We need underpants for mom, so that she will quit wearing dad's!" At this particular time I was pregnant and must admit that dad's were a lot more comfortable than mom's.

The Apple Doesn't Fall Far From the Tree

Mary Lou now has kids that certainly prove "the apple doesn't fall far from the tree."

Mary Lou took her three children to confession with her before Easter. The boys were old enough to receive the Sacrament but Alex, her youngest daughter, was only four. However, Mary Lou had no one to leave Alex with that afternoon, hence her being there. Alex was very familiar with the church surroundings because Mary Lou often attended daily mass with Alex in tow. She knew Sister and the Father well, and was insisting on entering the confessional first with her brothers and then with her mom. Mary Lou, in desperation, finally said, "Alex–No, I need my privacy!" Alex stood back, put her hands on her hips, and bellowed out, "Mom, you're going in there and take off all your clothes?"

Mary Lou used this expression, "I need my privacy, " when Alex would insist on going into the bathroom with her at shower time. Be careful what you say–anything can be used against you.

Watch What You Say

Sarah, my youngest daughter, definitely made a lasting impression on a counselor who was administering her psychological evaluation prior to starting kindergarten one year. As he emerged from his session with Sarah, I could not fathom the expression on his face. He looked straight ahead and refused to make eye contact with me. When I made it clear that I wanted some sort of explanation, all he would say was, "Watch out school!"

On the way home in the car I naturally questioned Sarah about the interview. Sarah proceeded to tell me that he had showed her a tree, asked her how many apples were on the tree, and she told him the answer. He then asked if she knew what a bouquet was and she said that she didn't. She called it a bunch of flowers. He then mentioned croquet, a word that she knew. After this he came up with another word that rhymed with bouquet and croquet. Sarah was not familiar with the word and replied that she did not know what it meant. She then asked him if *he* knew the meaning of the word and he answered "no," whereupon Sarah asked, "Why are you asking me if you don't know yourself?" Needless to say, Sarah never had any problems with school. She was always a good student and got along well with her teachers.

When Sarah was young, she did know a fraud when she saw one—you too, Lord? At times we all qualify—Don't we, Lord?

Life Can Be Colorful

This was the day Father chose to visit our prayer group. "Charismatic" was not his favorite word at the time. This I could understand, because for years I considered it most distasteful, perhaps in the same league with "conglomerate."

Corporations at one time were not highly favored if they were conglomerates. I was into my head at this stage of my life and did not understand any kind of religion concerning the Holy Spirit. It was nonsensical to me. Well, God took care of that!

Father was a holy man, a very straight, serious-minded individual. God decided He needed a few laughs and knew exactly where to get them. When I came into the prayer room that day I chose a seat directly across from Father. This was great except for the fact that I could not find two matching socks to wear when I dressed for mass so I opted for one red one and one green one. With long pants it didn't seem to be a problem, since they covered my legs quite nicely. No one would ever know. Unfortunately, when you sit down, pants tend to rise—Lo and behold! This, of course, is what Father beheld. He had no alternative but to gaze directly at his worst nightmare for the entire meeting. It blew him away. He could not take his eyes off those "awful" socks and I had a very distracted prayer meeting myself.

I was laughing on the inside about God's reinforcement of Father's already questionable attitude toward those wacky charismatics. As we departed I had to ask Father if he thought I was crazy. In a very serious tone of voice, he responded, "Yes, I certainly do!" To my knowledge, that was Father's only visit to our prayer group. He came, he saw, he left forever.

Kids Are for Real

My two youngest kids, a friend of my son's, and I were spending the afternoon visiting my daughter in New Haven, Connecticut where she attended college. Mary Lou was housemother in a three-story, old Victorian house. Her room was a converted sun porch on the second floor. While gazing out of the window of her bedroom, I was aware of a huge animal moving around on the porch next door. It took a few minutes for me to comprehend that this was a monstrous rat. His long, hairless tail gave him away. I called for my children to come see this impressive rodent. As they Ooh'd and Aah'd, their friend responded in a totally bored tone of voice, "Mrs. Drummond, we have bigger rats than that in our garage." This child's mother happened to be No. 1 citizen in our small town, an absolutely immaculate housekeeper. So much for one-upmanship!

While visiting my daughter, Nancy, in Oklahoma City, I picked up the newspaper one morning to see before me an article written about super large rats in New Haven, Connecticut. The town had released these neutered rodents in hope of decreasing the rat population. I can vouch for the super size, but not for the decrease.

Two four-year-olds were busy making a mess in my son's bathroom. An unwise mother had given them salt crystals to play with; the ones that develop into stalagmites when placed in water. As I was not happy with the situation, my voice announced this, emphatically. My son's friend responded by exclaiming over and over again, "Mrs. Drummond, I've got to go home right now! I hear my mother calling me. I've got to go!" (He lived within sprinting distance from our house.)

What came to mind was that this child had great potential. Could he possibly be a future president of the United States?

Please, Be Patient God

Eva was our next-door neighbor for many years, but was now living in New York City. Early one summer morning she appeared on my doorstep for a very welcome but unexpected visit. My project at that time was laying brick tile in the kitchen-utility room area of our house. Immediately after rising that day, I decided to do as much work as possible before it became too unbearably hot in the afternoon. You might say that I presented a very disheveled appearance: uncombed hair, bare feet, dirty hands and messy knees. My apparel consisted of a long night shirt displaying a picture of a crazy lady with the caption written in bold letters across the front, "Be Patient, God Isn't Finished With Me Yet." Eva was beautifully attired as usual—high heels, flawless makeup and so on.

After chatting with her inside we headed out the door to her limousine that was parked in the driveway. She was on her way north and had decided to pop in for a short visit. When the limo driver saw the two of us, the contrast was just too much to handle. Here was the "lady and the tramp" standing before his eyes. He died on the inside trying not to laugh on the outside. It took him a while to pull himself together in order to come around to open the door for Eva. "Be Patient, God Isn't Finished With Me Yet" was simply icing on the cake. Please God, hopefully you aren't finished with me yet? You were certainly starting from scratch that day.

Early Morning Rendezvous in New Hampshire

While on vacation in New Hampshire, our Ford truck needed servicing, therefore, I offered to take it early one morning to the Ford place in Franklin, a small neighboring town. After leaving the vehicle for repair, I decided to meander around the old factory town for the next few hours. While crossing one of the bridges in the area, I was stopped by a gentleman who wished to engage me in conversation. "Would you like to come home with me? I look much younger than I am." He told me that he was seventy-eight-years old and I agreed he did look a lot younger. He was in pretty good shape for an old geezer. Foolishly, I asked him how old he thought I was. He replied that I looked as though I were in my 60's. At that time I was in my 50's. My answer to going home with him was, "Buddy, you just blew it! I'm not going home with you!" Have you ever been propositioned at 8 o'clock in the morning and told that you don't look too hot for your age? I could tell God was really in need of laughs that day.

There was no morning mass in Franklin for me to attend, so I wandered around until 10 o'clock when I decided to drop into the church for a visit. Well, God was with me; there was a funeral mass in progress, which presented a great opportunity for me to receive Holy Communion.

As I entered and sat down in the back pew, I became aware of some highly disapproving glances that the ladies nearby were casting in my direction. Why, Lord? This went on for quite a while until suddenly it dawned on me that they thought I was some lady that "Ole Joe" knew that they didn't. It seemed unlikely to them that someone would walk in off the street to attend a funeral mass for an unknown person. In a little town everyone knows everyone else—if they don't know you, they certainly know everything about you. I became hysterical. There were only six of us who went up to receive communion but all seemed tuned into the stranger in their midst. No one wished to acknowledge my presence as we left the church. What came to mind was, "Ole Joe" had the last word that day and maybe forever. Who was she?

Just think, maybe I'm the only past Joe had. Could he have been a hen-pecked husband? God's sense of humor was pretty lousy that day.

Anywhere, Anytime

My destination was Oklahoma City. I had just finished chatting with a lady in the Salt Lake City airport who had shared with me her fascinating life story. On my flight from Idaho to Utah the gent sitting next to me had likewise related to me his interesting personal experiences. It looked as though this was not going to be a dull trip.

A young man had passed me in the airport and we had smiled at one another. When we boarded the plane it was a pleasant surprise to have him in the seat next to mine. He was carrying a large bag of books, which made me think he was going to school in Oklahoma. Actually, this was not the case. He was going to visit his dad in Oklahoma City, but he, himself resided in California. The literature he had with him was New Age material, a lifestyle he was currently exploring. I knew that I had to offer him some holy pictures and medals, which I had purchased at shrines in Portugal and France. When he saw the picture of Our Lady of Fatima he became very excited. This was the lady, he explained to me, who had appeared to him in a dream three weeks before. He eagerly accepted these tokens. It also occurred to me that I should offer him a rosary from Medjugorje, which I felt God wanted him to have. We entered into a discussion on how to say the rosary. In his younger years he had practiced Catholicism but now was searching for a sense of direction. As we were discussing the rosary I was aware that three people in front of us were straining to listen to our conversation. Two of them finally turned around and asked if I would repeat my explanation. They were Evangelicals who had been in Phoenix preaching. As we were conversing enthusiastically, a gentleman who was part of their group appeared and announced that he was hungry. My young male friend had a bag of fruit with him so he offered him a banana, whereupon, this individual wanted to know what he could do for us in return. I suggested he pray for us. He immediately dropped to his knees in the aisle of the airplane and commenced to passionately pray over me in a loud, clear voice. Silence reigned. I couldn't help speculating on what everyone was thinking at that moment. It was a great prayer too—very spontaneous and sincere.

Oh Lord, anywhere and anytime is fine with you. It should be fine with us too, right Lord?

Are You Listening, John?

Working in the shelter early one morning in Connecticut, I was aware that a young man sitting alone, eating breakfast was laughing to himself. No one was in a gay mood at 6 A.M. on a cold winter morning when they have to be out on the streets for the day at 7 A.M. It was most unusual to observe this sort of behavior. Finally, he looked up at me behind the counter and exclaimed, "You sure look like John Denver's mother!" Ha! Ha! Ha!

When we moved to Virginia Beach, after my husband's retirement, I was involved with the Legion of Mary and would go with the ladies for sick calls at De Paul Hospital. There was a resident nun who, the first time we met, laughed and laughed before finally saying, "You look just like John Denver!" If she were in the hall when we came into the building, she would grab me and anyone else coming down the corridor, literally accosting them with, "Doesn't she look just like John Denver?" It became quite a joke between Sister and the ladies who accompanied me.

On a pilgrimage to Poland, we had a Sister in our group who looked like someone I knew, but who, completely escaped me. It was very annoying, to say the least. After a couple of weeks of frustration, Sister took me aside privately one day and whispered, "Do you know, you look just like John Denver?" Bingo! Sister looked just like the Sister back in Virginia who would openly declare, for the whole world to hear, "She looks just like John Denver."

John Denver, I hope you're up there praying for me—your mother or your twin?

Clothes Make the Woman—or Do They?

In Kennedy Airport one afternoon, a lady from St. Petersburg, Russia, was eager to engage me in a conversation. She wanted to know where I came from. When I said that I was an American, she replied, "Never—You are not an American, because you don't look like any American I've ever seen!" We hassled back and forth over this issue until finally I asked her where she thought I was from. After much deliberation, she responded, "Australia," outback no doubt!

❀❀❀❀

On a pilgrimage to Spain an old lady in her 80's approached my roommate and I in the lobby of the hotel where we were staying. She stood there gazing at us for a few moments and then proceeded to ask me if I were Peter, our group leader. We became hysterical. This was too funny for words. I later asked Peter, "Where's your skirt today, Peter?" By the way, he was in his early 40's, with very dark brown hair and I was 65 at the time, wrinkled with gray hair. There was obviously a problem.

God had to have been desperate for a few laughs that day.

People Say the Darndest Things

My friend and I were browsing in a junk shop of a nearby town when we encountered a middle-aged man who was dying to share his life story with us. He told Jan and I that he was forty-five, divorced from his wife, remarried to a twenty-three-year old, had shaved off his beard and was now reborn. From what he had said we gathered he was a very successful artist who had a six-year-old son. As we were speaking about wives, children, etc., my friend declared, "Well, she has had seven." He stood back with a look of amazement on his face and exclaimed, "Seven husbands!" That was the nicest thing anyone had ever said to me—to think I could have gotten seven husbands.

We were travelling in the Holy Land between Haifa and Jerusalem when we made a rest stop in the middle of nowhere. As we approached the gift shop as well as the restrooms, we saw the owner sitting on a veranda watching us. His remark to me as we greeted one another was "Are you a nun?" I said, "No, I'm not a nun." He then explained that he liked my face and asked, "Are you married?" I replied, "I've got seven kids," to which he responded, "I didn't ask how many kids you had. I asked if you were married." When paying for my purchases, he informed me that he shouldn't even be charging me for these items. Maybe this Arab was looking for another wife who looked like a nun in his eyes—one of every flavor, you know!

A Steamy Adventure

We were on our way to the Royal Ballet performance at Rock Creek Park Amphitheater in Washington, D.C. Along the highly trafficked street my station wagon radiator suddenly decided to boil over. There was no possible way to get out of the long line of cars on either side of us. Since the production was starting momentarily, we drove into the wooded parking area, parked the car, which looked as though it were going to blow up any second, and hurried to our seats. We left folks standing around looking a bit flabbergasted. As smoke bellowed from the vehicle, we nonchalantly locked the doors and disappeared into the crowd.

In the midst of this great ballet, Nureyev was performing that night, I suddenly remember putting a cashier's check for a large sum of money in the breadbox at home. Our family had gone to the swimming pool earlier that afternoon and my last thought as I headed for the door was, suppose we have a fire in the house while we are away. It was a check for a considerable amount of money, one we were going to use as payment on a piece of property that we were purchasing the next day. That's when the metal box seemed like a great idea.

During intermission I hurried to the phone and called my husband. After explaining the situation to him, his only remark was, "What would you like me to do, put it in the refrigerator?"

After the ballet, we obviously had a problem—a big one. We were an hour away from home and it was eleven o'clock at night. The police officer directing traffic informed us that he did not know of any gas station nearby and he was not going to stick around after the traffic cleared out. People disappeared very quickly and there we were desperately in need of water. The only containers available for filling the empty radiator were a squeeze bottle and a bathing cap. Fortunately, there was a water fountain nearby. Three hours later we had completed our task as our cop "friend" chatted with us about his various experiences. He had decided not to abandon us after all.

As we headed for home in the wee hours of the morning we thanked the Lord for taking care of us and shared "a few laughs" with His Highness.

Johns Are Forever

On my first trip to Medjugorje in 1985, God had a real job for me to do—clean outhouses! There was no indoor plumbing near the church at the time. I was never a great housekeeper in the early days of my marriage; in fact, my role in life was to make other housekeepers look good. Bathrooms and kitchens suffered from my lack of enthusiasm. Decorating was my passion—not cleaning.

Since the Medjugorje experience, I have progressed to tidying up public bathrooms. Bits of paper thrown about must be picked up and sloppy sinks tidied. "Lord, save a soul." I once read that this was the job Mother Teresa chose to perform at the Motherhouse in Calcutta. God was allowing me to make up for all those messy bathrooms in my past, since travelling has been my lifestyle for many years.

On my 69th birthday, God presented me, courtesy of my friend Elaine, with a four-foot-high rustic outhouse. The interior contained four small holes for garden tools. It was a very fitting gift, in fond memory of toilets everywhere.

God's humor never ends.

Don't Pray for Me

This funny incident took place outside the grocery store in Ashton, Idaho. I had finished my shopping before my friend, Elaine, had completed hers. Sauntering outside to the parking lot I was greeted by a gentleman whom I had encountered briefly inside the store. He was obviously killing time also and wanted to chat. He told me he was a thirty-five-year-old bachelor wondering why the right woman had not come into his life. This topic he wished to expand on as well as his Mormon faith. We spoke about various things and one of the subjects he wished to discuss was how people dressed in Ashton and how come I had on a skirt, obviously making me different from everyone else (pants were the norm). I told him this was the way I dressed–period! He mused over this input for a short time and then Elaine appeared more than ready to head for home.

Our buddy had other ideas. He engaged us in conversation for forty-five minutes, leaning on the rolled down car window with his head half in and half out, so that there was no way to politely end the encounter. Finally, out of desperation, we announced that we had to go, but we would definitely pray for him. His eyes got as big as saucers. He stepped back and bellowed, "Don't you pray for me to become a Catholic!" His parting remark to me was, "By the way, I approve of the way you dress."

Seeing Is Believing

My daughter, Carol, invited me to attend a one-man show of Father Damien, the leper priest, at the Catholic High School in Louisiana where she taught religious education. It was supposed to be a very special presentation and I thought the idea rather intriguing. Since the gym was crowded that afternoon, they found a special seat for me close to the makeshift stage on the gym floor. I have a bad hip; therefore, not having to climb into the bleachers was a great blessing.

When the actor appeared on the stage in his long black robe and bushy beard, I naturally assumed that this was a priest or monk playing the role of Father Damien. His voice was absolutely perfect for the part and the acting was wonderful. It could not have been a more realistic performance of the priest's life.

After the drama was over, he spoke to the audience about his background, not a religious one at all, to my surprise. At the conclusion of his brief speech, it seemed appropriate for me to tell him how marvelous I thought his portrayal was. As I approached him, he turned to me, pointed his finger, and loudly proclaimed, "I know you!" To my knowledge, I had never seen this man in my life. He then continued to say, "You were in Medjugorje on the same pilgrimage with me." When he explained who he was, I remembered a clean-cut yuppie with a pink button-down shirt and loafers, whose wife was three months pregnant. They had been culinary art students together, were now married, and managing a ski lodge restaurant in Vermont. He was not Catholic, but his wife had talked him into taking the trip.

He then told me what happened to bring about his trans-formation. The Blessed Mother had communicated with him through her statue in the church in a very special way. After this encounter he returned to Medjugorje another time and hence his acting career. He also shared that he was able to support his family performing for God, which he felt was a miracle in itself. This sort of acting was not easy. Most of his colleagues were not as successful.

The transformation that I witnessed was pretty miraculous. God can do anything. Just say, "Yes, Lord, your servant's listening," and die to self.

Never Say Never

I was visiting with my daughter in July several months after having a hysterectomy. I was definitely on my way to feeling great once more—very feisty. My grandchildren loved the swimming pool. Grandmother, being addicted to the water herself, was joining the kids in all the summer fun at the local swimming hole. Diving off the low board seemed to be a great sport for all that morning and I couldn't resist the temptation to participate even though swimming laps was my forte and not diving off the low or high board. In fact, I made the statement that no way would I ever go off the high diving board. Heights have always bothered me. The thought of walking out unprotected onto a narrow little board high in the air was a terrifying one.

That afternoon we attended a movie, *The Empire Strikes Back.* In the movie, Yoda encourages Luke Skywalker to perform various feats of courage. As I watched, I suddenly became overwhelmed with the thought of having to climb the ladder and take the plunge. High dive here I come.

Sunday evening at 5:30 found my daughter's family as well as grandmother back at the pool. I was determined to attempt the scariest undertaking I could think of for the moment. Up I went, inching my way to the end of the board, where my feet absolutely refused to obey my brain. My toes curled around the end of the plank like grappling hooks and would not let go.

In the meantime there happened to be a young male behind me who was eager to get on with the show. I was finally able to remove myself from the end of the board so that he could get around me and do his thing. Walking back and forth on the board was becoming easier all the time, as the young male wished to repeat his leaps into the water. In fact, this entire procedure continued for forty-five minutes.

The pool closing time was 6 o'clock. The lifeguard, Steve, watched me intensely, while my daughter insisted, very strongly, that I come off the diving board. "My kids are hungry and Steve needs to go home. You know that you have to do it, Mom. Come on!"

The lifeguard asked her, "Who told her she had to dive off the high board?"

Carol promptly replied, "God told her so." Then Carol, who was a charismatic, began to pray in tongues. Steve wanted to know what she was saying and Carol replied, "I don't know what I'm saying." We now had big time intrigue.

All of a sudden I was aware that my daughter was now on the end of the high dive shaking like a leaf. She ran to the end of the board and dove off, something she had not done since her early teens. "Come on Mom, I did it, you can do it," was her retort.

Finally, I had become so comfortable walking back and forth on the board that I was able to go to the end and jump, not dive, but jump and then run up the ladder to jump once more for a repeat performance. Feet first has always been my style.

In the ballpark next to the swimming pool, I had somehow attracted attention and half the spectators were watching the screwy lady on the diving board. Will she or won't she? Place your bet folks!

Driving home from our eventful afternoon, Carol explained to me that she would probably die of embarrassment when confronted by Steve in the teacher's room that fall. They both taught at the same private school in town. However, when I questioned her later about whether he mentioned anything about the pool farce, she said that not only had he not mentioned the pool, but that she had become his trusted confidante.

Who would be surprised by anything if they had lived with such a mom he had encountered at the pool that summer? Are you surprised, Lord? Never say never!

Don't Miss the Boat

Driving home from Connecticut to Virginia, I stopped to visit with my friend in Annapolis. We decided that both of us could use a peaceful dinner at a local restaurant in the harbor area of the city. When we finished our meal, the evening was still young and a nice harbor cruise seemed like a great idea. We strolled over to where the boat was usually docked but there was no one in sight. As we sat waiting, trying to decide what our next course of action should be, a water taxi appeared and the driver asked us if we were looking for the cruise boat. Our response was "yes." He said that it was in the middle of the river but he would take us to it. We got into the small craft. As we left the dock area he spotted several other people who were obviously looking for the ship also. He returned to pick them up and we continued our voyage into the middle of the Severn River.

Since there was a strong wind blowing, boarding the vessel was not easy. With the waves rocking the taxi as well as the boat, one going up while the other went down, one had to jump at the exact moment. Thank goodness the people assisting us knew what they were doing.

The lady who greeted us as we came aboard asked where we were from. I answered Connecticut, and my friend responded Annapolis. Grinning from ear to ear, she exclaimed, "We're from Allstate!" She then explained to us that this was the Allstate Insurance Company cruise. They were out for the evening so we should not plan on going ashore for another three hours or more.

If we were looking for fun that night we had found it—a

cruise up the river with dancing, food, and drink. My friend made the statement that she hoped there was no one on board who knew her. When she returned from getting our drinks, she said that the young woman bartender asked, "Oh, Mrs. Doe, what are you doing here?" She was a friend of her daughter's so much for anonymity.

We had a rollicking good time that night. As we were leaving the cruise boat, I thanked our lady greeter and told her what a wonderful time we had experienced, whereupon she rolled her eyes and exclaimed, "I know!"

I have a feeling two old ladies may have been the floor-show for the Allstate Insurance Company cruise. A good time was had by all—courtesy of Allstate and God!

Peace on the Jersey Turnpike

My mind was actively hooked up like a broken record replaying over and over again the thought provoking incidents, which had taken place at my mother's funeral. We were headed north along the New Jersey turnpike to Connecticut and I was asking God to please give me peace. "Come on God, turn me on to some other channel." In my rearview mirror I happened to notice a car that seemed to be following me. If I moved into the right-hand lane, he followed me. If I moved to the far left, he was right behind me. Two of my daughters were with me, Mary Lou, who was married and lived in New Haven, Connecticut and Sarah, my twelve-year-old. They were both sleeping soundly. After an hour or so of observing my pursuer, I awakened the girls to see what they thought was happening. I sped up, went around numerous cars, and sure enough there he came, my "ole buddy," a lone male in a large car. He was not going to allow me out of his sight.

Sarah announced that she needed to use the rest stop so as soon as one was sighted I cut over quickly to exit and "Charlie" did likewise. This was a very unnerving situation, a bit frightening for all of us. Mary Lou suggested that we drive up to the front door instead of using the parking area since Sarah was the only one who wanted to get out of the car. Our friend pulled up parallel to my vehicle, rolled down his window, leaned across the front seat and shouted, "Are you going to New Hampshire?" We happened to have New Hampshire license plates on our car. He then related to us that he had been broken down on the highway for hours. When we went by, his engine had just been repaired and he needed to be in New Hampshire by the following morning for a preaching engagement, but wasn't sure how to get there. If we were going in that direction could he possibly follow us? His dilemma was that this was late in the afternoon and he didn't know how to navigate the George Washington Bridge. Traffic was fierce at this time of the day. We explained to him that we were going to Connecticut via the Garden State Parkway and the Tappan Zee Bridge but he was more than welcome to follow us. In fact we planned to stop for dinner along the way and extended the invitation for him to join us, which he readily accepted. He was a charming twenty-seven-year-old who belonged to a religious singing group in Delaware and was conducting a workshop in New Hampshire right over the Massachusetts border. Generously, he offered a tape, which the group had made, to Mary Lou. It was a very professional recording.

When we adjourned to the ladies room I suggested to Mary Lou that it might be a kind gesture for her to offer him lodging for the night. She lived close to the Connecticut throughway, which would make it simple for him to travel to his destination the next day. She responded that David, her husband, would only say, "Here buddy, take this $30 and go find yourself a motel." I asked her weeks later if she ever approached David as to how he would have reacted if she had brought the stranger home. She said yep, and that David had replied, "I would have given him $30 and told him to find a motel." (This took place over twenty years ago when motel rooms were a lot cheaper then.)

God certainly answers our prayers, usually in unexpected ways.

Life's Greatest Moments

Since I have mentioned working at the shelter in Connecticut, I must make the statement here that one of the greatest New Year's Eve's I ever experienced was celebrated in the Norwalk shelter kissing all the street people. It was a wonderful gift for my friend Jan and I.

On another occasion, while serving folks at the Soup Kitchen, a young male dressed unbelievably in a sequined black shirt, black silk pants, black velvet tam, and jazzy shades, swaggered up to me as I was preparing food and surreptitiously pointed a knife at my side. He informed me that he had just gotten out of jail. Into my head came the thought that after having seven kids terrorize me for years, this dude definitely was not going to get any reaction. I just chose to ignore the gesture. Pretty soon, in the course of our conversation he was saying "yes Ma'am," "yes Ma'am," "yes Ma'am."

One of the people in charge of the place approached me later and remarked that I had a real calling for the Soup Kitchen.

God Works in Mysterious Ways

At age twenty-two, I married an unbaptized male who had little religious upbringing. He was special in so much as he would say the rosary with me when he was home from one of his frequent trips across the Pacific. Being an Air Force transport pilot, based in Hawaii during the 50's, he was gone most of the time, however, when at home I would insist that he attend church on Sunday, any church was fine. We happened to be living on Waikiki and the Baptist church was only a block away from the Catholic church, so exercising his right to freedom of choice, sometime he would attend my church and then occasionally he would go to the Baptist church. It was not easy for him to remain anonymous with the Baptists. They had him stand up and identify himself—who he was, where he came from and so on. My husband, being a very private person, found this procedure somewhat embarrassing, therefore, he preferred the Catholics who could have cared less who he was or where he came from.

Several of the Baptist ladies appeared on our doorstep one Saturday morning and wanted to know where he had been. They had not seen him in a while. He explained to them that he often flew to Japan, and was not in town very much. The Korean War was in full bloom at this time. He also mentioned that his wife was a Catholic and sometimes he attended the Catholic church with her. One of the visiting ladies inquired as to whether his Catholic wife ever attended the Baptist church with him. His answer was "no," and very indignantly she wanted to know, "why not?"

Soon after this incident, which my husband felt was an invasion of his privacy, he asked me about taking instruction to become a Catholic and he became a convert shortly thereafter. I always give the rosary and Baptists credit for this conversion. He simply prayed himself into the church with an extra boost from some well-meaning, over-enthusiastic Baptist ladies.

❀❀❀❀

A few years later, while visiting his mother in the States, mom asked what church he was going to attend that Sunday morning. He informed her that he had become a member of the Catholic Church. She immediately wanted to know, "Why the Catholic Church?" He reminded her that she had always said she did not care about what church he went to as long as he went. Her immediate response was, "I meant any church but that one!"

Could mom and those ladies have had a similar calling? Here I am Lord!

Is Someone Listening Down Here?

On the TV sitcom *One Day at a Time,* Ann (Bonnie Franklin) and her mom were having a wonderful discussion/argument while seated in the middle of a restaurant having lunch. As their voices started to rise so did the attention of those seated nearby. Pretty soon, there was a riotous argument in progress with various bystanders choosing one side or the other. It was truly a funny show.

The next evening my husband and I decided to eat at a local restaurant, which was amazingly empty even for a Monday night. We ended up being seated next to a couple who were having an extremely animated conversation concerning their divorce. I know that we did not speak more than ten words to each other the entire evening. The dinner talk next to us was just too absorbing (better than the TV show the night before even though we opted not to take sides).

Thursday found us at a restaurant in an adjoining town. My two youngest kids were visiting their sister in California, so it was an ideal time for us to eat out. This particular evening I chose to relate to my husband my spiritual journey, a most interesting one to say the least. He just happened to be too mesmerized to turn me off, which he usually did. As I became more animated in describing some of the rather unusual things that had transpired in my life, I noticed out of the corner of my eye that the people seated next to us were strangely silent. They had terminated their conversation and were definitely straining to listen to my story. They had even moved some of their chairs closer to our table. Everything goes full circle, so they say. God was definitely enjoying the merry-go-round that week.

❀❀❀❀

Mary Lou and I once entertained a businessman during our luncheon in New Haven. We discussed some thought provoking subjects during the meal and had a bit of an argument going too. I asked the gentleman as we left if he enjoyed the luncheon floorshow and he admitted that he did. Why didn't I hold out my hand at least for a small contribution or are the most exciting things in life free? God, for instance.

What You See Is Not What You Get

Climbing the Mountain of the Apparition in Medjugorje at 3 A.M., I felt led to prostrate myself in front of the large wooden cross, which was located against the well-trodden path that continued up the hill. Upon reaching the cross, which marks the spot where the Blessed Mother originally appeared to the children, I sat down, positioned my back against some rocks facing the candlelit area, and started to say my rosary. There was no one else on the mountain at this time. It was extremely peaceful until 4 A.M. when a man appeared who was most interested in checking all the petitions that had been left for the blessed Mother. I had the feeling he was looking for money. He did not see me at first as I was tucked away from his view with my all-purpose coat hood covering part of my face. He finally caught a glimpse of me back in the shadows, approached me with his hand outstretched and grunted. He obviously did not speak English but his strong body language made it very clear he wanted something. I offered him the rosary but he shook his head and continued his gesturing. I then thought it might be my flashlight by my side. It obviously was because he snatched it out of my hand, turned it on, poked it in my face and reacted with a loud, disgusting "Yuck" and jumped back.

I must say, I had very mixed feelings about his reaction to my appearance. Could I have really been that awful to behold? He then returned my light, ignoring my presence as he continued his search amongst the paraphernalia near the cross.

At dawn, another gentleman appeared, whom the intruder likewise approached, but for a cigarette. As the late arrival and I departed from the mountain together he told me about one of his companions on a previous pilgrimage who had been raped in Medjugorje (the devil is certainly alive and well wherever God happens to be, demanding equal time if at all possible).

Returning to my room, I entered my bathroom and looking in the mirror I burst into laughter. There, all over my face, was red mud. In prostrating myself before the cross I had gotten dirt on my face and in the progress of rubbing off bits and pieces of clay I had managed to smear this stuff all over my skin.

God saves in most unusual ways. We laughed together, He and I. It did make me feel better, though, about the "Yuck." My husband says I was rape-proofed.

Bells Are for Ringing

Father was speaking at the Sisters of Notre Dame Motherhouse in Wilton, Connecticut. He had just told his audience that his community was in dire need of a bell. Their old bell had developed a crack and was no longer in use.

At the end of the week, I was going with my husband to Savannah, Georgia for several days. He attended a flight simulator refresher course twice a year in the area and this time I was to accompany him. Into my head and out of my mouth simultaneously came, "Good heavens, I'm going to Georgia to find a bell!" The gal seated next to me exclaimed, "If anyone can find one, it's you." What a crazy thought. I put it aside very quickly.

Strolling around down by the waterfront in Savannah, my husband and I passed numerous stores amongst which was an antique shop. As we walked by, into my head pops the crazy bell business. I told my husband, just so I could dismiss all thoughts of finding such an item, that I was going to poke my head in the door and ask if they happened to have what Father needed. This was definitely not the kind of shop that would have a bell—I was almost sure. I was absolutely right. However, they recommended a big antique-junk shop in another part of town, a location too far for us to walk to that evening. Thank goodness.

The next morning as we were driving out of the city headed for Hilton Head, my husband suggested that we stop by the place mentioned the night before. "It just happens to be on our way," he said. I reluctantly consented. It was a huge Quonset hut structure crammed full of items.

You name it, they had it. As I walked to the back of the shop, there resting against the rear was a large bell. I could not believe God would do this to me, however, I should have known better. When questioned, the dealer announced that it had just come in the previous evening. How do you get a big, heavy bell from Savannah, Georgia to Sedona, Arizona? Ship it, of course! The shop clerk said that the dealer across the street would be more than happy to crate it up and send it to Arizona. We were not talking about a cheap endeavor, not for the purchase or the mailing. The person who would be in charge of shipping was not to be reached that Saturday morning. We would have to get in touch Monday for particulars. Where would we ship it? I did not have the faintest clue as to an address. Then I remembered the only thing that I had in the rental car was their bulletin which I had picked up at Father's talk and brought along to read. This had a very vague Sedona address on it. Needless to say, the bell was supposedly on its way to Arizona when we left Savannah.

After procrastinating for two weeks at home, I decided that I'd better send a letter to Father announcing that a bell was on it's way. A week later I got a letter from him stating that they had a bell ringing in their hearts and their minds, but no bell in sight.

My husband was on a trip to Bermuda when I got a phone call from his secretary saying that a man in Savannah was trying to get in touch with Speight about a bell. I got the number from her and found out that the bell was in Phoenix but they could not reach anyone concerning the exact location of the community in Sedona. "If you do not come up with a more explicit address by this evening, the bell is on it's way back to Savannah," I was told. This was 9 o'clock eastern standard time and I had to take immediate action. I called Arizona information only to find out there wasn't any phone number listed for their community.

Where does one go from there? I called the local church and Father told me he hadn't the faintest idea where they were located. I called the local Post Office that gave me an 800 number that connected me to the Postal Department in Hartford, Connecticut. They told me they could care less about a bell in Arizona. Finally, it occurred to me that just maybe the number was listed under Father's name. Bingo! When I contacted information, they had a number. The phone rang and rang until finally someone answered, saying that they were just passing by the building and happened to hear the phone ringing. I did talk to one of the priests who informed me that the town had protested about their street sign. Although they took it down, another one was in the process of being made. However, there were two large developments along the road and their community was located right between the two. "If you suddenly find yourself in the other housing area, you've gone too far," was his retort. He did offer to stand down on the road (long robe and beard) so that the delivery truck couldn't possibly miss the turn off.

I called Georgia once more and relayed this crazy information. The response was, "Lady, I refuse to fax all these wild details out to Phoenix so you had better come up with something else—quick." Thank you, Lord, that there was a two hour time difference between Arizona and us. Around five o'clock my time, after mulling all of this over and waiting for my husband to call from Bermuda, I tried calling Sedona once more and reached one of the nuns who offered to call the freight company in order to give them better delivery instructions. Enough is enough, Lord!

My husband called later and remarked, "Good grief, you're dealing with people just like yourself." I had a policeman come to my door one day wanting to know why I had 81 Hillbrook as my address instead of 21. When we moved in I had a great brass number eight and number one to put on the signpost at the end of our road so it seemed perfectly alright to put this up with the understanding that I would black out part of the 8 making it a 2. I just never got around to it.

Later Father told me that the bell was responsible for their moving to Colorado. Sedona had become crowded with retirees who wished to sleep in the morning. Someone wrote an editorial, which appeared in the local newspaper, that this bell was a menace. It had to go! They did not move to Arizona to be awakened early every morning by a loud clanging bell. As the community had been contemplating a move for quite a while, due to the encroachment of civilization in their surroundings, this decidedly was an added incentive. They had to go as soon as possible.

What would one expect from a ship's bell in the desert? It had to go.

Mistaken Identity

My daughter Carol was visiting us in Idaho and one afternoon we decided to make a pilgrimage to Our Lady of the Rockies in Butte, Montana. We had only traveled thirty-five minutes down the highway when a car pulled out into our lane. Carol swerved, missing the other vehicle by inches, a thrilling way to start our journey. When we arrived in Butte we were too late to take the bus to the top of the mountain, but we found an area where we had a great view of Our Lady and proceeded to do our praying of the rosary and made our visitation from that vantage point.

It was getting dark as we left the mountain and headed down the highway into Idaho on a very deserted road. Going seventy-five-miles-per-hour with smashed bugs covering our windshield, we came upon a huge white Pyrenees dog in the middle of the highway, totally confused, darting first in one direction and then the other. Carol, there again by the grace of God, swerved at the right moment missing the confused animal. (People in the West carried their dogs in the back of their pick-up trucks. Sometimes they fell out, as this one obviously had; there was a truck pulled over to the side of the road.) Our Lady was showing us just how much she was looking out for us.

We had stopped at a Subway shop for a couple of sandwiches a few miles back from where we had our exciting moment. It was a blessing that we had decided to wait to eat until later. As Carol said, "Thank God I didn't have a sandwich in my hand when we encountered the dog." Thank God the dog was big and white.

Finally, I got my sandwich out and ate it, but I had misplaced my daughters. When we stopped along the road to clean the bugs off the windshield we found her food between my seat and the door. As she proceeded to eat hers, half way through the sandwich, she exclaimed, "I hate to tell you this mother, but you ate my sandwich!" I'm a vegetarian and had ordered a cheese veggie sandwich, Carol's choice was a turkey with cheese and mustard, but all she could find after devouring half of the sandwich was cheese. I was aware of the mustard but thought I wouldn't comment on the fact that I had not told the lady to put mustard on my sandwich. We became hysterical. There were no adverse affects from the turkey, just plenty of laughs, which we both needed at that point. God too, most likely I wondered why that sandwich tasted so good!

Your Will Be Done

My daughter, Sarah, was in New Zealand as an exchange student one summer. The curriculum included not only staying with a family and attending school, but a four week wilderness adventure. It was July and I had stopped to visit my friend Lou in Dover, Massachusetts, when in the course of the conversation she mentioned that retirement for her was coming up in another year-and-a-half (she was a child psychologist at Tufts). A colleague at work had inquired, "What is the wildest thing you might like to do after leaving your job, Lou?" Lou responded, "Go to Calcutta and work with Mother Teresa!" (for Christmas one year, I had given Lou a book by Mother Teresa that she said really impressed her). Whereupon the lady responded, "Why don't you?" Her dilemma was who on earth would she get to go with her? It wasn't an adventure she wished to take on her own, Out of my mouth came, "Oh I'll go with you, Lou." I felt as though I had shot myself. Her immediate reply was, " I'm going to hold you to that." All I could think of was that Sarah was having her outward bound in New Zealand and I was going to have mine in Calcutta. If you're as big a chicken as I am, you can imagine how the thought of going to such a place struck terror in my heart. The best thing I could do was not allow myself to think about it. One-and-a-half years was far in the future. However, I had the uneasy feeling that God was going to hold me to my Fiat.

When I asked my husband for his input on this venture of ours, his response was, "No way am I giving you any money for Calcutta." He went on to explain that years before he had visited a center in Africa for the study of African communicable diseases. It was an appalling experience for him. As they were leaving he expressed his feelings to one of the doctors whose reply was, "If you think this is bad, you should go to Calcutta!" Hence my husband's negative attitude and apprehension toward any member of his family spending any time or any of his money in such a seemingly God-forsaken place.

Well, time passed. It was October 1987. I called Lou inquiring whether she was still serious about our Indian adventure. She replied that she had not changed her mind. I told her that I would approach my husband again and keep in touch. Speight's reply when I informed him that Lou was serious about going to India was, "I'm just as serious about not giving you any money." "OK, God, if you want me in Calcutta, you're going to have to cough up the money." I have to be honest; it didn't matter to me one way or the other. The thought was just too scary.

It was Sunday morning when all of this transpired. Sunday night I got a phone call from my brother in Annapolis telling me we were getting some money from an obscure will, a cousin had died and we were inheriting a sum of money.

The Drummonds were in the process of moving from Connecticut to Virginia at this time and I was in Virginia getting a condo ready for our first relocation in more than eighteen years. It came to my attention that there was bingo at the local church school cafeteria on Monday nights. Since I was alone and hadn't played in years, it seemed like an amusing way to spend the evening. Maybe I was supposed to win the $1,000 jackpot? No money had been forthcoming from the will, so maybe God had "Bingo" in mind as a means for me to be able to pay for my ticket to Calcutta. Needless to say, that was not his intention.

I returned home much poorer and less sane than usual.

Bingo was no longer as I remembered in the past. Playing nine cards at one time was a bit much for a novice. It wasn't cheap either. Calling my husband in Connecticut late in the evening, I was told that a letter had arrived from a lawyer in Maryland. Would I like him to open my mail? Naturally, the answer was "yes." Can you believe? It contained a check for $5,000. Sounded like the loaves and the fishes to me. Why think of a measly $1,000 when He can increase it fivefold?

There was a young person with me in Nova Scotia who had belonged to Mother Teresa's contemplative New York group. Through her connection with the Sisters of Charity, my husband and I met Sister Nirmala, now back in Calcutta. I felt very strongly that we needed to get in touch with Sister for information on where we might stay if we came to India. My friend, the former nun, had Sister's telephone number in Calcutta so I called her one evening. It was 8 A.M. in the East and miracle of miracles Sister came to the phone (that phone never or hardly ever worked to my knowledge, the entire time we lived in the compound). She gave us the information we needed, including the name of the Sister we were to contact about possible housing. Suddenly, it occurred to me that I must ask her if we should come at all. There was dead silence on the end of the line for what seemed like an eternity and then she responded, "Yes, do come!" I felt as if God were issuing an order. When I related the conversation to my husband, he had to have been extremely impressed because from that moment on he was telling everyone that his wife was going to Calcutta.

Why argue with God? He always has the last word.

Come as You Are

Back in Connecticut, it was a Monday morning when I remembered that a good friend's father-in-law had died and that day was the funeral mass at the local church. When I went out to get in my car, it wasn't there. One of the kids must have taken it to school that morning leaving me with a big Ford truck, full of garbage destined for the dump. We had a tag sale at our house over the weekend and all sorts of unsaleable items were piled high for future disposal. This presented a dilemma; no other transportation was available. To go or not to go? I went.

After mass, cars queued up for the cemetery and my truck was the last in line. The family of the deceased was quite formal in their approach to life. They drove in Cadillacs. I laughed to myself as I joined the procession. Coming up to the stoplight where the policeman was directing traffic, I was not allowed to follow the cavalcade to the cemetery. The indignant cop blew his whistle and threw up his hand for me to stop.

After he vanished to complete his morning duty, I drove up to the cemetery, where I was greeted by the very same peace officer with a perplexed look on his face directing traffic, including garbage trucks into the cemetery. A few laughs, Lord!

No Trespassing

Monday morning my friend, Elaine, and I decided to visit the local abortion clinic. We were simply going to walk up and down the sidewalk saying the rosary. As we strolled in the back of the building, we were interrupted by a guard who informed us that we were on private property, our car as well as our bodies were trespassing. He was calling the police. Since I had my first encounter with the cops in Maine, I was not quite as upset as my friend's face told me she was with her first threat of being sent to jail.

When we went to move our car, however, we discovered we had locked our pocketbooks inside and the car keys as well. Locating the guard, we related to him our dilemma, but he would not allow me to use the phone to call my husband to ask for his help. He couldn't believe that I had the nerve to ask. What to do? He was still telling us that the cops were coming, and there was no key and no money to make a phone call.

We went across the street to a service station where a very kind lady took pity on us two destitute ladies and allowed us to use the phone. While we were awaiting my husband's arrival, sure enough, we saw the police arrive at the clinic, fortunately, we were nowhere in sight. After a seemingly endless period of time, they left.

When my husband arrived, I put on one of his hats, pulled it down as far as possible over my face, donned a pair of sunglasses, and took off to recover my vehicle, which was doomed to be confiscated at any moment. I now knew exactly what a car thief felt like. You sure get a rush of adrenaline!

Junking Can Be Hazardous

It was a beautiful summer day for meandering through the Northeast countryside. My friend Lou and I were on our way from Dover, Massachusetts to her get-away in Maine. We both had problems passing up good junk shops, garage sales or some of those broken down abandoned houses that one might encounter in that area of the state. One particular disaster caught our eyes and we decided to explore the ruins. Inside was a total mess, stuff thrown all over the place, garbage stuff. Upstairs in the attic were no floors, only a big beam that Lou bravely crawled across in order to rescue an old trunk. There was little else to be had.

We proceeded to the barn, which also was empty except for a few hole-filled baskets. Since we had been traveling for a long time, Lou decided to go out behind the barn for nature's calling. I strolled out towards our car only to be greeted by a police car in the driveway and a cop announcing to me, "Lady, anything you say can be held against you." At that moment I knew that I should have joined Lou behind the barn. My bladder just couldn't stand the excitement. It was a good thing I happened to have on white pants. Out of my mouth, to my surprise came, "My kids always did say this might happen to you someday, Mom." He was not amused. He proceeded to tell me that only weeks ago he put three men in jail that he caught trespassing on this same property. They evidently had a trailer that they had loaded with furniture. There certainly wasn't anything like that left in the house, that's for sure.

When I first saw the cop car I called to Lou and told her

there was a policeman out front but she didn't believe me. She now appeared on the scene, speechless. In my mind she was going to be the spokesperson for the group, because she was a pretty loquacious person. I've never seen her at a loss for words, a very charming lady.

Well he wanted the car registration, and I couldn't help laughing thinking about poor Harry, Lou's dad, who was now the receiver of stolen goods, unbeknownst to him. We had decided to use his vehicle for our trip because neither one of our cars was in great shape. The cop made us open the trunk where we had stashed the trunk from the attic and a few other worthless items. He proceeded to put them in his car. Under these circumstances I felt incredibly silly. It was either weep or giggle. The cop had no sense of humor whatsoever and when he finally got exasperated enough with us, he simply said, "Ladies, get in your car and don't you ever come back here again." Out of the corner of my mouth, again to my surprise, came, "Oh no, Lou, the next time we return, you'll have to wear a different color wig!" This was greeted with one blank stare from our "friendly" local cop.

As we drove down the road, the first words uttered by Lou were, "Whew, what I need now is a good chocolate soda!" Then she started to giggle and pulled out some old postcards from her purse. These were part of the garbage strewn about on the floor. I laughed and came forth with an old cellulose brush. We had an adventure, and a close call, and God most likely, a few laughs.

So What! In Colorado

I was attending a seminar on Buddhist Christian dialogue at the University of Colorado in Boulder one summer. It was the great world semantics contest; word play was rampant amongst the participating intellectuals.

One evening in the garden a lady reporter and I were chatting before the 8 o'clock lecture. We were engaged in a very animated conversation about what had been presented previously, when I interjected, "You know, the two most important words in the English language are So What!" She seemed speechless for a moment obviously not agreeing with my remark.

Our speaker that night was a Buddhist monk who was a very spirit-filled man. He would make profound statements during his talk, laugh like crazy, and then exclaim, "So what!" He repeated this expression at least six times. God truly must have been chuckling.

In this crazy world of ours the only true entity we ought to take seriously is God. If you sit and ponder these facts you might realize that we're all a bit nuts and we shouldn't take ourselves and others quite so seriously.

The Blessed Mother Giveth and the Blessed Mother Taketh Away

I received a beautiful Czechoslovakian gold and pearl rosary from my friend who visited her homeland each year. A lady present at my prayer group meeting asked me if it was pure gold. This was exactly what it appeared to be however, I replied that I didn't think anyone I knew would send me a gold rosary. The chain on my beads broke soon after I started using it, so. I placed the rosary in a basket on my dresser in hopes of getting it repaired in the near future. My preference was definitely for the cord rosaries since the chain ones fell apart very quickly for me; apparently, I'm not a gentle rosary user. We were in the process of moving from the West to the East Coast and when I went to empty the basket on my dresser of its contents, there were two pieces of perfectly silver colored rosary beads. I've heard of many rosaries turning from silver to gold, but never gold to silver.

I found a silver-colored rosary at a tag sale for a dollar. The beads, as well as the rest of the rosary were the dull color of ballbearings. I couldn't pass up a rosary for a dollar, so I bought it. When examining it at home, I discovered in tiny letters on the cross that it was sterling silver. In attempting to polish it I was not happy with the results so there again I tossed it aside for future use. One day in going through my drawer, I discovered a "glowing" silver rosary. It has been glowing ever since—it never needs polishing, never tarnishes. You just knew I liked silver better than gold, Blessed Mother—or at least you hoped so.

Remember, If You Can

Since it was golf tournament time again my husband's friend, Hugh, from North Carolina was visiting us. He decided to take an afternoon nap, but suddenly changed his mind saying he needed to go to the Commissary first to pick up various things for his wife. Checking my refrigerator I realized I needed orange juice, milk, and cottage cheese, which he generously offered to include on his shopping list. Asking him if he would like me to write down these items he said, "Heavens no, I can remember what you need." As he repeated numerous times—cottage cheese, cottage cheese, cottage cheese—he then proceeded to tell me a joke about a man whose wife sent him to the store for oranges, apples, and bananas. When she suggested she write them down for him, he declined saying there was no need because he could remember very well what she wanted. Returning home with eggs, bread, and coffee, his wife exclaimed, "Where's the bacon?"

I was resting when Hugh returned from the store. When I came back to the kitchen to prepare dinner and opened the refrigerator door, I beheld orange juice, milk, and sour cream.

"Where's the cottage cheese, Hugh?" I asked.

"Well you know, my wife is always asking me to get sour cream," he replied. Our memory is not what it used to be, is it?

❀❀❀❀

During my husband's last visit with his friend in North Carolina, he was told another wild tale of a memory lapse. Hugh and his wife had been cleaning out the garage when he realized he needed to go to the hardware store to purchase several items. Unable to find what he was looking for at the local shop, he proceeded to Wal-Mart where he made his purchase and returned home one-and-a-half hours later. While in the kitchen, he heard a tap, tap, tap and hastened to the front door, but there was no one there. Back in the kitchen once more, he again heard the same sound. This time he checked the garage door and found his wife safely tucked within. In his haste to get to the hardware store before closing time, he had managed to lock her in the garage. Fortunately, she had found ice cream in the freezer and old newspapers to keep her pleasantly occupied during his absence. I did ask Hugh on his last visit if he checked his garage before he left home.

Moments of Revelation

Halloween night my husband returned visibly shaken from house hopping with our two-year-old Sarah. He remarked, "She is going to be sick." After showing me the empty bag I questioned him as to what happened to all the goodies, knowing we had very generous neighbors. He explained that Sarah was firmly convinced she had to eat everything given to her as soon as she received it. Mom obviously had made an impression by insisting her daughter eat all of her dinner before getting any dessert. It was impossible to make her understand otherwise. Sarah's capacity for sugar was enormous and hasn't changed much over the years. The apple doesn't fall far from the tree, does it? (Since her mom also is a sugar addict.) By the way, Sarah didn't get sick!

❀❀❀❀

Carol, our sixteen-year-old, was driving home from her job at a local swimming pool in a thunderstorm. When approaching a red light during the deluge she applied her brakes but to no avail. The car did not stop as she expected but hydroplaned into the vehicle in front of her. She then attempted to get the driver's attention by knocking on his window. He seemed to be in a state of shock gazing heavenward, totally unresponsive to her banging. Finally he saw her and opened his window to see what the problem was. After she told him what had happened he announced, "I thought thunder struck me!" There wasn't any damage to his car but the front end of ours was a mess.

Returning from college in Oklahoma to Connecticut for the Christmas holidays our daughter Barbara lost her suitcase at the airport in New York. I received a phone call from a gentleman who lived several towns away saying that he had picked up her bag by mistake and could I meet him on Route 7 where he would gladly deliver the missing luggage. When he appeared, I was nonplussed by the expression on his face, as well as those with him. When Barbara opened her suitcase, I could not believe my eyes, it was filled with rags! Everything had holes, big holes, particularly in the dungarees. It was the style then to wear such apparel but this was definitely carrying fashion to an extreme. No wonder the puzzled looks on the faces of all the people in the car. I would have loved to have been there when this man originally opened "his suitcase." Barbara then made a remark that she had asked a friend to come and spend the holidays with us, however, the girl's response was, "I don't think your family can afford to have me for such a long period of time, Barbara." Maybe we couldn't, if we had to replace all of Barbara's rags. Today Barbara now has a daughter who gives her moments of concern about her choice of clothes. Full circle is definitely the name of the game.

❀❀❀❀

Nancy as a teenager had insisted Speight, her dad, construct a bed for her that was fastened to the ceiling by ropes and swung like a hammock. It was a pretty ingenious creation—you simply didn't dare move in your sleep. Barb, working for a modeling agency in New York, brought a photographer friend home to spend the night. Nancy's room was the only one available at the time, so he was gifted with a unique experience. The next morning when I inquired if he had slept well, he replied, "I was seasick all night long!" Would you believe this was the first and last visit?

Who Sent You?

Filling out the information form for my new dentist I was asked, "Who was my referral?" We had lived in the area only a short time but I had obtained a dentist's name from a friend however I couldn't find it when I needed to make an appointment. I decided to simply pray over the names in the phone book to see what I could come up with. Having successfully used this method in the past, I found it to be a valid means of locating a good physician, why not a dentist? We've moved around a good bit lately and its proven to be workable. While in the dentist chair, I became aware that he was reading the information from my questionnaire. He suddenly exclaimed, "God sent you here!" "Yes," I said, "He was my referral and you had better live up to his expectations!" He rolled his eyes and said, "Oh Lord!" You can't find a better referral than God, can you?

✤✤✤✤

While waiting for the dentist to appear I was engaged in a conversation with his assistant who mentioned that the dentist was planning to marry one of his hygienists in the near future. This gentleman was a divorced, attractive, middle-aged male who had a successful practice and an exciting lifestyle. His fiancée was in her early twenties. The whole situation seemed a little crazy to me. I know that young women who fall for middle-aged men are more likely to be impressed by their money and position rather than their irresistible charm. When the doctor appeared I just had to say what was on my mind, since I knew him quite well from my frequent visits. "She is marrying you for your money and experience Doctor!" In the meantime his assistant is jumping up and down saying, "Yes, yes, that's right. Oh Lord, I'm going to have to take my valium after this because he's going to let me have it for days." She kept repeating how she felt and I couldn't resist expounding on the subject while he was drilling on my teeth. To make a long story short, the next time I went back to see him, about one-and-a-half years later, his assistant told me they were now divorced and she really did have to take her valium. By the way, my filling fell out two years later, but it was worth it. Sometimes you just have to say it as it is!

I Am, but I'm Not

After a Sunday Mass the lady sitting in front of me, whom I had never seen before, turned around and asked my name. When I told her Nancy Drummond, she exclaimed, "Oh, that sounds like an author's name," and she kept repeating, "Nancy Drummond, sounds just like the name of an author to me." I mentioned I was writing a book about God's sense of humor. She then invited me to join her for coffee and doughnuts in one of the adjoining rooms where many other parishioners gathered after mass. My husband was playing golf so I was free to accept the invitation. Entering the room I found my new friend, with her husband and an elderly gentleman, who motioned me to sit down. In the midst of a very animated conversation the lady suddenly exclaimed, "You and Mr. Doe are perfectly suited for one another. You have got to get together!" The gentleman, a widower for several years, was a jovial chap and we were bantering back and forth at the time of her outburst. I then had to inform a disappointed lady who was playing matchmaker, I had a husband, very much alive, just out to golf!

All That Remains

There are some very interesting stories that are told concerning where people keep the ashes of their loved ones or perhaps, not so loved ones? They may be placed on a mantel, in a closet, or a really wild location such as an ice cream carton in the attic. My husband would no doubt approve of the latter, as he's always complaining about the ice cream he just bought disappearing from the freezer. Since there are only two of us in residence, most of the time, it isn't hard to figure out where it went. I did tell a friend who had her husband's ashes safely tucked away in her closet, and wanted him in her casket, we could perhaps purchase an extra large bra and stuff it with her deceased husband's remains. It's certainly one way to take him with you. No doubt, hanging onto the remains of one's spouse can mean in some instances, now I've got you right where I want you! To me, cremation can best be described as maggot deprivation. What fools we mortals are–God has to be laughing, or possibly weeping at our incredible stupidity!

Doing It Your Way

My daughter was attending a kindergarten presentation at the local school. Tricia, her five year old, was on stage gleefully singing, "She'll Be Coming Round the Mountain When She Comes." All of a sudden Carol hears her daughter's words, "I won't be eating chicken and dumplings when she comes," instead of, "We'll all have chicken and dumplings when she comes" with everyone else. Questioning Tricia later as to why she changed the words to the song, Carol was told, "I hate chicken and dumplings!"

Tricia always did her own thing and when young would often wear her dresses backwards with different color socks. Carol was stopped by a lady one day in the grocery store who thought it was a terrible thing to allow a child to express herself in such a manner.

Of course, her grandmother had a dress that was made from a feedsack that had been sent to Peru, emptied of it's contents, fashioned into a dress and sent back to the United States. I loved it and wore it frontwards and backwards, as well as occasionally wearing mismatched socks, so much for family eccentricities. It was here at Carol's, while observing my grandchildren, that I realized "the apple doesn't fall far from the tree." It was a real revelation to me at the time. We often ask, "Why are those kids like that?" Guess!

Expect the Unexpected

One of the nicest gifts God ever gave me was a truly remarkable experience as I was getting ready to depart from a stay at the Phoenix Desert Retreat Center in Arizona. It was a wonderful spot and during a past visit I saw coyotes chasing a rabbit by my door, hawks soaring for hours, and quail scampering through the desert fauna several times a day. While finishing breakfast before leaving I complained to God about a lack of animal entertainment this visit when suddenly I became aware of a loud cawing near the hermitage deck. Going outside I was greeted by a raven who flew right side up, upside down, right side up, upside down. Turning around he once more repeated his performance. This was an unforgettable climax to a great retreat with you, Lord. Thanks! He was a crow who was truly doing it his way.

We received our son Chris' first report card from his kindergarten teacher stating, "This child shall never be led!" We weren't sure if this was supposed to be a positive or negative statement concerning our son. Later when we questioned the teacher she assured me it was a positive observation. He was not influenced by his peers then or as far as we know, ever.

At a very early age Chris trained white mice to ride in his toy cars. He wanted drivers for these autos and would place the small critters in the driver's seat and squeeze them whenever they tried to escape. Eventually if their cage was opened they would dash for the cars without any further instruction. He taught those mice how to do it his way.

Mistaken Identity

Nancy Fowler, a visionary from Conyers, Georgia, was speaking one evening in Ridgefield, Connecticut. At that time we were living in Virginia; however, my friend Ann generously offered me a place to stay while in town when I decided to come for her speaking engagement. Remaining near the entrance of the hall where she was to lecture, I was greeted enthusiastically by many old friends. Out of the corner of my eye I could see a lone male standing a short distance away who kept gazing at me with an enamored look on his face. Finally it was time for Nancy's appearance and most of the incoming crowd had taken their seats when this same man suddenly approached me and asked, "Are you Nancy Fowler?" I replied, "No," and he responded, "You look just like I envisioned her to look." I guess to him one Nancy looked just like another Nancy, right Lord!

❀❀❀❀

Father greeted me before Mass one day, in the same church where Nancy Fowler had spoken, with, "How are you sister?" I realized by the expression on his face and by the remark of the person who accompanied him that they thought I was a nun. After his homily Father asked all the mothers in the congregation to please stand, which I did. Laughing to myself about God's "rotten sense of humor", it was very amusing to observe Father's face as he beheld the "nun" who was a mother and a grandmother.

❀❀❀❀

My friend, Marge, told me that she and her fourteen-year-old daughter were walking through a large shopping center parking lot when Jean exclaimed, "There goes a man dressed just like Mrs. Drummond!" It was a monk in his robes. My wardrobe at that time contained a long brown cape that certainly could have qualified me for a housewife appearing in monk's clothing. I'm sure it wasn't exactly the fashion statement I wished to make!

Many years ago on the beach in Waikiki, Hawaii, I was approached by some beach boys who were cavorting near by. "Are you a lady wrestler?" they asked. Some lady wrestlers had just arrived from the mainland and the newspapers were making a big production of the event. My husband got teased occasionally by me about the fact that he married me for my muscular legs, which God didn't give to him. Some get, some don't, Right? God! Let's keep it in the family anyway.

My husband certainly has other attributes. A very serious-minded lady who lived across the street from us during our Air Force days once remarked while we were having our morning coffee, "I have only met two men in my life that I could be married to, your husband and mine." Back then I wasn't so vocal as I am today–I was speechless!

Another person who lived next door told me that when a young neighbor of hers asked who had given her the new tea set she had just acquired she replied, "My boyfriend did!" Whereby the teenagers asked, "Who, Mr. Drummond?" I've also had women announce that he was the best looking male they had ever seen. A neighbor across the street in Hawaii used to tell me what great legs my husband had. It's all in the eyes of the beholder. You can't have it all–so much for muscular calves in your legs, Speight!

Gifts to Remember

While walking around my daughter's college campus on a September afternoon, I became aware of a young squirrel who was having the time of his life. He would toss a small stick into the air, turn a somersault, and catch it. This action was repeated numerous times as he joyfully threw himself up into the atmosphere and captured his play toy.

❀❀❀❀

A mother raccoon with her babies in tow regularly visited our summer cottage in New Hampshire. We would place food in the backyard for her; therefore, she came daily to partake of our generosity. One evening when I went outside to bring the dish into the house for refilling, a young raccoon appeared, who ran up to me and attempted to climb my bare leg, eager for the small amount of food left in the bowl. He wasn't easily dissuaded and his determination was a bit frightening to say the least. Raccoons have sharp claws. Finally I was able to escape from my captor, relatively unscathed, but it was a thought provoking experience that ended our feeding of wild animals. Remember, don't feed the animals!

❀❀❀❀

My daughter Sarah and I were looking out of the glass door that opened onto our screened porch in Connecticut, when we saw a tiny mouse scamper across the cement floor and hide himself behind a piece of barn siding that lined the porch beams. He caught sight of us silhouetted in the early morning light and disappeared behind the board, but apparently could not believe what he saw. Slowly a small head rose above the board with two tiny eyes peeking at the monsters in the doorway and quickly vanished. He repeated this action numerous times before finally taking off in terror from where he came. These "monsters" were too much for his little brain to comprehend. Can you imagine how large we appeared to such a tiny critter? Dinosaurs on the loose, no doubt!

Loons were always a very special attraction at our cottage on the lake in New Hampshire. I can remember hearing them in the middle of the night when I was alone and thinking how frightening it would be to listen to their cry if you weren't aware of what produced this startling sound. Could it be a pack of wolves howling in the distance?

I was busy straightening our condo on the beach in Ocean View, Virginia, when suddenly I heard the cry of a loon, a sound that filled me with overwhelming joy. There in front of our building swimming amongst the waves was a loon. I had never thought of loons being in this area even though I knew they spent the winter on the Atlantic Ocean. It was quite a gift. Thanks Lord!

Food for Thought

Hurrying to make some cookies for the kids, I had produced the strangest looking oatmeal cookie dough I had ever seen. My oldest daughter, Carol, appeared in the kitchen as I was contemplating this weird concoction and remarked, "Mom, don't you think there should be oatmeal in oatmeal cookies?"

❁❁❁❁

My friend Lou and I were busy making rum balls for the Christmas holidays. By the time we got through stirring, tasting, and molding repeatedly, neither one of us could do anything more than giggle. Bombed by the balls, not cannon balls, but rum balls.

Drinking was never our thing, therefore it didn't take much. Thank goodness!

❁❁❁❁

A group of ladies were gathered for lunch and it was time for dessert. I could not resist the chocolate concoction at this particular restaurant and made the statement I might possibly sell my soul to the devil for a chocolate cookie. (I knew better than to make such a statement.) The next evening found all of us at our weekly prayer meeting when one of the ladies who hadn't been with us for lunch the previous day, wished to share with the group a dream she had had. Entering a church for prayer she was greeted by a statue of the Blessed Mother that suddenly came to life. Mary descended to where she stood, took her by the hand and proceeded to walk by her side. Kathy had much to say but could only ask Our Lady what she should do with her life. Mother's response was, "Give up chocolate!" Since Kathy had a great deal of chocolate stashed away for the holidays, this really struck a chord. Upon awakening she knew she had to get rid of it all. How's the chocolate addiction in your life?

Where Do You Go From Here?

I was never a great seamstress. I've only made five dresses in my whole life, three of which were corduroy jumpers with blouses for my girls when they were young. For someone who believes that nothing is impossible with God, I offered to make two prom dresses for my daughters. These were ambitious projects, particularly since the black gown was constructed from a complicated Vogue pattern with wide cuffed sleeves and numerous small covered buttons. Five o'clock the night of the prom, I was still in the process of finishing off the details on these creations. God was good. The girls were pleased, and "mother" was surprised by the finished product.

A year later I received a phone call from my neighbor, an illustrator of book covers who was in dire need of a dress that would be appropriate attire for the actress, Eva Marie Saint, in a New York Times movie ad. The film was about Hitler, starring Alec Guiness, and she was playing the role of Eva Braun, the Fuhrur's mistress. The only dress I could think of that might be appropriate was the black creation in the closet. Victor came! He approved and there in a full page ad of the New York Times appeared my dress. Where does one go from there? That was the end of my sewing career except for a million pillows constructed for our various homes and a few curtains.

God sure has a great sense of humor. How many strive all their lives for a full page ad in the New York Times? I was never a great seamstress!

❀❀❀❀

One morning before going to work at the homeless shelter, God was really calling attention to the fact that it was ten degrees fahrenheit outside and there were those who needed extra warm clothing that day. It seemed imperative to me that if there were any items in my closet that could be used, they were to be taken now. I prayerfully hoped that I was choosing the right articles of clothes as I grabbed a multitude of items from the closet. There was no time for head decision making; God had to provide. One article in particular happened to be a sheepskin cape that my husband had given me as a present several years before. It had to go! A week later I received a few phone calls from friends asking, "Have you seen the front page of the Norwalk paper?" The answer was, "No!" They told me one of the street ladies from the shelter was pictured wearing my leather cape. God is good—sometimes he likes to advertise. I later saw the picture which was a huge one-—Sadie had good taste. She had certainly impressed one reporter!

Oops, Sorry!

Mother Angelica had just announced San Francisco was having an earthquake. I was busy cleaning my daughter's kitchen after all the children had gone to school, when I heard this news broadcast coming from their TV in the living room. Since my daughter Barbara was living in Larkspur, located very near the Bay area, I immediately got on the telephone to see if it was possible to contact anyone there. My son-in-law answered the phone at 6:30 A.M. seemingly unaware of any such catastrophe. However, after my animated description of what Mother Angelica had reported, he was convinced it might indeed be taking place. After hanging up the telephone and listening for further details, I realized the program was a re-broadcast of what had happened months earlier. Since I had been traveling in China when the California disaster occurred I was unfamiliar with the particulars.

It wasn't easy to call my son-in-law back and apologize for my foolish mistake. My daughter was swimming in San Francisco Bay at the moment, therefore when he called her club concerned about an earthquake his mother-in-law said was supposedly taking place, they assured him this was not the case. There were a lot of laughs that morning, but not from Mark, who has still not forgiven me for my boo-boo! How unsettling can one's mother-in-law be?

We all make mistakes and some of them can be very humorous. Shortly after our arrival in India we were spending a night in a hotel in Calcutta and had made several unsuccessful phone calls to the States. My friend Lou was anxiously awaiting a return call from her kids when at 4 A.M. a beep, beep, beep, sounded outside. She drowsily reached for the phone by the bed and said "hello, hello, hello," but no answer was forthcoming. I was laughing as I announced, "Lou, it's a car down in the street." She hung up the phone and went back to sleep. Several hours later, again beep, beep, beep, was heard and once more Lou picked up the phone and said; "hello, hello, hello," no answer.

Those cars were giving Lou a ray of hope but not much else, and me a few laughs early in the morning.

A group of ladies had just finished a birthday lunch at the Chamberlain Hotel in Hampton, Virginia. We went outside to await our ride back to Norfolk when, because of the cold blustery weather we opted to return to the lobby. Entering the building the automatic door refused to close even as we moved back and forth it didn't respond. Finally in desperation I said, "JoAnn, take my walking stick," which she did and as she waved the cane and uttered "close," the door closed. She said, "Open." The door opened. Repeating this at least five times, with the door responding to each command, we all laughed uncontrollably. It was like Moses opening and closing the Red Sea!

Looks Are Deceiving

A friend in our neighborhood never failed to remind me that she was younger than her husband and me. He happened to be my age but several years older than Sue. All of us were in our late thirties. While shopping in town one afternoon we decided to stop at a furniture store for a particular item she was interested in buying. As the salesman greeted us he asked if he could be of any assistance to her and her "daughter." The expression on my friend's face stopped him dead in his tracks. Wide-eyed he stammered, "You and your daughter-in-law?" I happened to have a scarf around my head that day but it certainly had to be God's sense of humor—just waiting to have the last word with Sue!

Lou and I seemed to shop at the local junk shops quite frequently. We both had large families, I had seven children and Lou had eight. Therefore it seemed to be a wise thing to do. The store manager approached one day inquiring if he could help her and her daughter. Every once in a great while someone would ask if I was Lou's daughter and we would burst out laughing. (I hope she laughed.) She happened to be ten years older than me.

Many years later while junking in New Hampshire with my friend Jean, the man in the shop asked if I had my "daughter" with me that day. She happened to be ten years younger than me. God had just been waiting to bring this saga full circle and you know it wasn't that funny when I was on the other end of the stick!

My friend Andy and I were attending a Lenten seminar that was based on the life of St. Francis. The minister who was sharing the role of moderator with a Catholic priest was not terribly pleased with some of my comments. After the lecture was over, we chatted very briefly with him and he inquired if I were a teacher and where did I teach. When I replied no to his question, Andy interrupted with, "Oh yes, she is! She teaches in the front seat of her car." A deep silence followed this remark.

Monsters on the Loose?

Chris, my grandson, just recently told his mom when he was very young, two or so, he would awaken frightened in the middle of the night, get out of bed and head for her bedroom. However, such awful snorting rumbling noises issued forth from the room, that a terrified Chris did not have the courage to enter there. As he scampered back to his own bed, he knew terrible monsters were loose where his parents slept. He was not quite sure whether they would escape the beasts and be alive the next morning. Have you had any monsters loose in your bedroom lately?

Carol who was getting ready for a Christmas party one night, had her teenage daughter, Lisa, arrange her hair and apply makeup in such a way that she looked at least ten years younger. Five-year-old Elaine entered the room and aghast at the results quickly vanished from sight.

When Carol appeared in the living room ready to go, her husband inquired, "Who is this woman? I've never seen her before in my life." Elaine had coached her dad into saying this to Carol, in order for him to be in total agreement with Elaine's absolute disapproval of her mom's transformation.

As Carol entered the party that night, she was greeted by one of her husband's associates who obviously did not recognize her. When he approached her later at their dinner table, she announced who she was and he was flabbergasted.

In Elaine's eyes this was a "monstrous" transformation of her mom, while everyone else Ooh'd and Aah'd. Beauty is truly in the eyes of the beholder.

Candid Camera, Where Are You?

Several ladies were busy helping me pack one morning during our move from Virginia to Arizona, when suddenly I heard a faint voice calling for help. "Help, Help, Someone please come and help me!" As I glanced around the living room, I saw two little legs emerging from within a large box and frantically waving in the air. Somehow my friend had fallen head first into the container as she attempted to pack some items in the bottom of the huge carton. The packers, who were busy hauling things to and from the moving van, passed her on either side but chose to ignore it all. Finally, after realizing they did not intend to come to her rescue, I went over and pulled Elaine out of the box. I would love to have been a fly on the wall that night when the movers discussed their day. Do you think she might have momentarily considered a cheap trip to Arizona and then changed her mind?

Never Out to Lunch

On a plane heading for Medjugorje, Yugoslavia, I was seated next to a young lady from a neighboring town who related to me a very funny story.

Her husband was a contractor who had been unable to sell a house he had recently constructed. It was not a builder's market at that particular time in the 80's, therefore, with small children to support they were most anxious to rid themselves of their burden. She decided to offer God $1,000 if he would allow them to sell this home. Miraculously, a buyer appeared on the horizon.

While attending a healing service in Greenwich, Connecticut, the lady made the decision to present God with the $1,000, however, at the last moment, she wrote a check for $500 instead. The healer, Amazing Grace, suddenly announced from the stage of the auditorium, "There is someone in this audience who is trying to cheat God out of $500." Needless to say God received his check for $1,000 in the collection basket. He is never out to lunch and wants his money up front. Amazing Grace is amazing!

Have You Been Bugged Lately?

After receiving Holy Communion at mass one morning I suddenly felt a bug crawling inside my shirt. Shortly afterwards another one made his presence known in the same area. What popped into my mind was all the Japanese beetles I had been removing from my rose bushes were seeking revenge! Early each morning, I collected these critters from my flower garden. Usually they were dropped into a jar with a tightly fitting lid, but this day the container was inside the house, therefore, I used a plastic bag that happened to be in my skirt pocket. Unfortunately it was not a zip-lock model. As I intended to dispose of the pests immediately, this did not seem to present a problem, however, I am easily distracted and I forgot.

Heading for home across the meadow after mass, I discovered a nearly empty plastic bag in my pocket. My husband could not possibly understand how anyone could forget a pocket full of beetles. I can, can you Lord?

Bugged by the bugs!

Dumps Are for Picking

My son Chris and I had a lively debate early one morning at the local dump. Before taking him to school that day I needed his help in order to drop off some heavy rubbish at the town refuse center. There laying on the ground near our parked car was a pile of wonderfully weathered barn boards, some of them split or broken, obviously why they were discarded. At the time we were busy giving the interior of our house a touch of rusticity by installing old beams and old wood paneling inside. My mouth watered at the sight of these wondrous boards, free too, an added plus. Chris was not one bit enthusiastic with our find so he protested mightily when I insisted he load the station wagon with my new found treasure. Pretty soon there was quite an argument going on at the local dump. I threatened not to take him to school until he put the boards in the car and he emphatically stated he wasn't going to since they were worthless in his sight. Finally mom won and we hauled three quarters of our loot home.

After dropping Chris at school I hurried back to pick up the remaining goodies after calling the doctor to cancel my 9 A.M. appointment. There was simply a more pressing matter to be taken care of at the local dump that morning. Eventually we paneled our living room wall with the barn boards and were able to construct a great fireplace hood out of the remaining bits and pieces (metal lined of course). Would you believe that Chris now married bought this house when we moved to Virginia and he himself chose to live with the "disgusting trash" for at least ten years.

Sarah, Dick, and I headed for the dump one summer morning in New Hampshire. We had bought a small cottage on a lake that we were busy furnishing. There were still a few items we needed to purchase in order to finish the project. I had told the kids we must to go to town that day and buy a lamp, a rake, and a tool for the wood stove. Before that it was necessary to dispose of some trash at the dump. Driving into the area, we had to wait for a truck in front of us to dispense with their garbage before we could dispose of ours. As they drove away we spied a practically new rake on the ground beside our car. Sarah jumped out and grabbed the unbelievable find. When I went to throw my bags into the trash heap I was greeted by a remarkable lamp resting at my feet and off to the right was a perfect fireplace tool. Who needs to shop in town when God is giving away freebies at the dump?

When we moved back to Virginia, I was in need of various items to complete the decorating of our house. Some lady friends had suggested one of the discount stores but it occurred to me that I should try the local junk shop first. One of the things that I was looking for was another yellow pillow for the sofa. I had purchased this particular pillow in a discount shop in Phoenix, Arizona, but it was an unusual shade of maize so I didn't believe it possible to successfully match it here. There at the Salvation Army used merchandise outlet was the exact pillow, brand new! Unbelievable, but not for you God. Looking for a vegetable bowl to complete my set of china I discovered a dish that perfectly matched the ones at home. The dump or the junk shop Lord? Free or almost, is a great way to go!

To See or Not to See

While attending college many years ago I was asked to model some clothes in a fashion show being presented for the student body. There was one small problem for without my glasses I could not see very well. An understatement to say the least and the thought of having to navigate a series of steps leading to and from the stage was a terrifying one. No way would vanity allow me to be wearing spectacles the evening of the performance. My guardian angel worked overtime that night. Somehow, we seem to qualify for God's help despite our own stupidity.

❀❀❀❀

The eye doctor had become a close friend of mine since I frequently visited him as a teenager. He would generously dye my eyeglass frames if I wearied of the current color. After trying them on for a final check before leaving his office, I would then remove the spectacles and place them in my pocket. I might add that this was all before contact lenses were perfected. The doctor remarked to me as I was leaving one day, "How on earth do you find your way home?" I didn't know how, but I always did–thanks to You, Lord!

❀❀❀❀

It could be extremely embarrassing not to be able to see especially when I attended dances at the Naval Academy. After leaving the ladies room and walking up to the wrong fellow on several occasions, I gave my escort for the evening explicit instructions to grab me as soon as I emerged. How were you supposed to recognize your date when everyone was dressed the same? You see one midshipman, you see them all, particularly in a dimly lit room and without my glasses, of course. I would have worn my specs but that would have required overcoming vanity and depriving God of another opportunity to lead the blind, right Lord!

After my marriage in Great Falls, Montana, we were on our way to the West Coast. Waiting in the airport were several other Air Force personnel who were pretty fresh after their afternoon liquid refreshments. Returning from the ladies room, can you believe I walked up to their table and sat down? They thought it was great but my husband was not a "happy camper." I must say I was a bit distressed by my blunder. Enough is enough! Lord, surely my husband's Air Force career could have been cut short if he had punched out some major.

I learned that swimming underwater doesn't help my vision one single bit. In the Pacific Ocean while submerged I tweaked the wrong gentleman. Oops, not my hubby!

Doctors Say the Darndest Things!

When I was expecting our first child in Hawaii, the doctor at Tripler Army Hospital said to me, "Lady if you have a boy, please don't name him Speight." (This happens to be my husband's name.) There also was a physician at the hospital who would not allow anyone to see their babies if they weren't willing to nurse them. He remarked, "If God wanted you to do otherwise, he would have hung two milk bottles around your neck."

❀❀❀❀

My OB-GYN doctor in Connecticut had a real gift for memorable remarks. When I first went to him he exclaimed, "Lady, women who come in here either expect me to be their father or their lover." I never did ask which he thought I wanted him to be. I was too shy thirty years ago.

When I phoned him at his office while having labor pains his secretary told me he was outside pouring cement. Calling me back later his comment was, "You know cement and pregnant women never wait for any man!"

❀❀❀❀

After reading my chart the doctor wished to know why I had gained weight. I announced it was because I had been eating a lot lately. He then remarked, "You're the only person who has ever entered my office and said they gained weight because they've been overeating. Most people tell me they simply cannot understand why they have a weight increase. It's never from stuffing themselves!"

❀❀❀❀

The OB-GYN doctor at the Air Force Base in Florida remarked to me in 1956 after his examination, "You're 28 years old and that's too old for having babies." Today that's a pretty amazing statement for most people and for me too, since my last child was born when I was forty.

After having Sarah I was visited by the doctor who sat smoking in my room. Entering with my newborn, a nurse saw the smoke and quickly headed out the door while my physician exclaimed, "A little smoke never hurt anybody!"

❀❀❀❀

An Indian doctor friend who had listened to me for years when I went to see him about my constipation commented, "This is exactly why you're so full of it!"

❀❀❀❀

After seeing a doctor at Yale about my hip, I was greeted by the remark, "Stay away from doctors," as I prepared to leave his office.

❀❀❀❀

My four-year-old grandson, Zack, went with his mom to the pediatrician for his annual physical. The doctor first asked him if he had eaten a good breakfast that morning and he replied, "No, just some junk food." His mom said she kept her mouth shut (a monumental thing for my daughter to do). Her remark to me was that he had eaten three breakfasts that morning. The doctor proceeded to examine his ears and when he was finished offered the instrument to Zack to look into his ears. Zack's comments after checking one of the physicians ears was, "Boy, do you have a lot of carrots and potatoes in that ear." Upon examining the other ear he stated, "Nothing but carrots in that one." Next the pediatrician/psychologist examined Zack's mouth and throat and again offered Zack the opportunity to do the same which he did commenting, "You certainly didn't brush your teeth this morning," whereby the doctor retorted that he certainly did. Zack said, "No way, not with all that black and brown stuff in there." The doctor tried valiantly to defend himself, telling Zack they were coffee stains, which he refused to believe. Now it was shot time and after receiving his first one Zack quit screaming long enough to announce matter of factly, "You told me it wasn't going to hurt." Then proceeded to scream again until he quit long enough to announce, "You didn't tell me the truth, it does hurt!"

Don't Be Late

Father gave a very animated homily one Sunday evening about people being late for Mass. He was extremely distressed, that we, I being one of the guilty ones, could not be on time for the 6 P.M. service when he had been at the Philadelphia airport at 4 P.M. and was still able to be there on schedule. He even announced he was going to make all the guilty ones stand up so the whole congregation would know who they were. I really wanted to rise for the occasion but chickened out at the last minute.

Sharing Father's story with several ladies at lunch a month later when one had announced how angry another priest was at late arrivals, it occurred to me that Father had signed, sealed and delivered himself to be late.

The next morning at 8:30 A.M. Mass there wasn't any priest. Ten minutes later one of the parishioners went back to the sacristy to check out the situation. Upon returning, she announced that Father had overslept. Twenty minutes later he sheepishly appeared. When Mass was over I felt called to ask him if he remembered his indignation at the late arrivals a month ago, and told him what I had said the day before. He replied that God does have a sense of humor and my response was, "If he didn't, he would have wiped us all off the face of the earth a long time ago!"

The bottom line to this story is the next morning I was late and had to take a seat right in the row in front of Father in the small chapel. God never misses a trick. He has the last word and I had set myself up!

The Lord Giveth and the Lord Taketh Away

There have been a number a wedding rings in my life starting with the original wide gold band that my husband presented to me on the day of our nuptials.

After a brief stay in Great Falls, Montana, we resided in Honolulu, Hawaii for four years. Shortly after our arrival on the Island, we were swimming in the Pacific Ocean when a huge wave came, knocked me flat, while the undertow painlessly removed my ring. At this period of time in our lives we were not affluent enough to replace the lost band as we were still paying for my engagement ring. Returning to the mainland after my husband's tour of duty with the Air Force, I discovered a temporary replacement at a pawn shop for ten dollars. This proved to be a cross since the skin under the ring continually peeled off and I was only able to wear it for special occasions. Eventually we bought matching wide gold bands, but unfortunately the results for me were the same.

Vacationing in Virginia with Speight's mother I mentioned to her what I needed was a narrow gold wedding ring. I couldn't say wanted because I had always preferred a wide band. In the course of our conversation his mom mentioned she had two such items in her jewelry box. Would I consider one of them? When she brought forth the rings she explained the more attractive narrow band she had found on the beach by the Atlantic Ocean. The Atlantic giveth and the Pacific taketh away! After wearing the ring for a couple of years it too vanished in a pile of woodchips at the town dump. What's the message, Lord?

Dandelions Are Forever

St. Therese, the Little Flower, says we are all flowers in God's garden and we all have a purpose.

While praying on the Rosary Hill at La Salete Shrine in New Hampshire, it occurred to me to ask God what kind of flower was I in His garden. At the time I was praying a Hail Mary by the Glorious Mysteries. When His response to my question was a dandelion, I looked down and discovered I was kneeling in a multitude of these blossoms. From that time on dandelions have taken on a whole new meaning in my life. I have found them everywhere in the world, except China where they're most likely eaten as soon as they appear. The amazing thing about the plant is that you really cannot get rid of the "weed" easily, if at all, and certainly many people feel this way about me. The seeds blow everywhere. You can make dandelion wine or use the greens for salad. They are an herb and can be used for medicinal purposes. One friend reminded me that I told her to buy a house we were looking at because there was a dandelion blooming in the front yard in December and a cardinal sitting in a tree. She did decide to buy the property which proved to be a most enjoyable living experience for her whole family. When I encounter a dandelion in an unexpected place or at a strange time of the year I feel that it is God saying, "Hi, here I am!"

Not long ago I was waiting for my friend in her car outside a bank where she had gone to inquire about a loan. There in the earth close to the vehicle was a fully mature dandelion plant with three large blossoms, an unheard of phenomena in New Hampshire on April 8.

Since dandelions entered my life in a very meaningful way it has been most difficult for me to remove them from my yard, without real pangs of conscience, particularly those encroaching on the driveway or coming up between the cracks in the cement walk. I remember quite clearly a monk friend saying to me, "I've tried everything I know to get rid of you, but I can't, so it must be providential." A dandelion always returns if possible and hopefully with God's blessing.

Carjacking

Exiting Wal-Mart one evening in Corpus Christi, Texas I looked for my husband and daughter who were supposedly waiting in a rental car at the curb. We were in a rush to return to our friend's home where her husband was not expected to live through the night. Quickly I opened the back door of an auto parked at the entrance of the store, hopped in, and positioned myself behind the driver of the vehicle. When I looked up expecting to see familiar faces, was I surprised. In the front seat sat a lone male behind the wheel, who was gazing into his rearview mirror with a totally petrified expression on his face. He was speechless and I was dumbfounded until I regained my senses enough to apologize for being in the wrong place at the wrong time. Crawling out of the car, I left my still "mute friend" trying to comprehend what had happened to him. The carjacker came, he saw, and vanished. Thank God!

I came out of church one Sunday morning in New Hampshire, after chatting with a friend for several minutes, and expected to find my husband patiently waiting for me with the car engine running. Approaching the vehicle, I reached out to open the door but it was locked, therefore I began to vigorously pound on the window, not at all happy with this situation. Slowly the tinted window opened partway and there seated in the driver's seat was a startled stranger who looked at me with a bewildered expression on his face. I exclaimed, "Gee I guess I have the wrong car. It certainly looks like ours." He then told me he was waiting for his mom, but he had seen my husband's auto, which had been parked in front of him. He had to move in order to let him out of his parking space. Then he stated, "Your husband just drove off lady." After my attack on his car, I guess he understood why. I laughingly responded, "At least I've made your day an interesting one!" A strange lady determined to get into his vehicle could not have been an everyday occurrence. By the way, my husband had gone to the service station several doors down from the church which is where I thought he perhaps went. Church can be exciting inside as well as out!

❀❀❀❀

While visiting relatives in Virginia beach I started out early one morning expecting to locate the local Catholic Church in time for daily mass. I had been given directions before I left the house but somewhere along the way made a wrong turn. Traffic was heavy, therefore, I pulled over into a left-hand turning lane at a stoplight and quickly hopped out of my car in order to get further instructions from the occupant of the auto in front of me. After approaching the vehicle, I became aware that the male driver was refusing to acknowledge my presence. As I tapped on the glass, he looked at the ceiling, fiddled with the dial on his radio, and straightened papers on the seat beside him. Finally out of desperation he cracked the window and stared wide-eyed at the intruder or perhaps the carjacker? When I asked about the church, he simply shook his head but never uttered a word. Dashing to the car in back of me, I received the answer to my dilemma from a kind lady who did not feel threatened by the could-be assailant.

Once Is Enough

I went through a period in my life where I was really considering the possibility of reincarnation. During this time many funny happenings occurred which certainly didn't point to a previous existence of notable acclaim. Approaching my husband one day I asked for his thoughts on the matter, whereby he replied, "You were just an old prostitute and not a very good one at that." While visiting my OB-GYN physician, we somehow touched on reincarnation and he retorted, "I know what you were—an old prostitute!" (Speaking of two minds working as one.) God had to be laughing that day.

A monk friend of mine did believe in reincarnation and after our first meeting I had this wild image of how we had known each other in a previous life. We were both drunken male Indians out West who were so enamored by old trunks, boxes, and the like, that we couldn't resist robbing stagecoaches. We later sold our loot to the local fence, for a bottle of booze, after painfully relinquishing our treasures.

Speight's cousin arrived at our house one afternoon from Virginia and announced he had this great vision of me as he drove up the highway. In years past I was the Abbot of a monastery who could have cared less about my monk's spiritually, only about running a tight ship. I know that I have a pre-disposition for money, therefore, God has always shown me when I get tight fisted how quickly it can disappear and things fall apart. I tell my husband if you want it you'd better give it away. For us this seems to work, if it's God's will!

❀❀❀❀ ,

Another funny scenario took place in the Wild West also. My friend's husband was a bartender in a saloon and she was the madam of the house. I was one of the call girls. (Can't get away from being that old prostitute, can I?) I do not believe in reincarnation today. Thank you, Lord! When I die I hope to go back to Him and not back to the Wild West. By the way, we've lived there and it's still wild!

Cars?

One evening I received a phone call from an agent with our insurance company in Texas, wanting to check with me to be sure the information they had was correct. As he named off the various vehicles designated on the policy I could understand his perplexed tone of voice on the other end of the line. It sounded like a used car lot as he enumerated six old autos, a Pontiac station wagon, a Volkswagen, a BMW, a 240Z and so on. All of these were well past their prime. I didn't have the nerve to tell him that my husband had rented a car that week in order to get to work because none of them were running. After this experience we purchased our first new car in twenty-one years of marriage!

Arriving at the airport in Virginia one rainy evening, my friend and I rented a car but were having difficulty getting it started. Our windshield wipers were going, the lights were on, and the radio playing but the engine would not run. After winding down our window, not a pleasant task in a cloudburst, we were able to get the attention of the attendant who dashed over to see what our problem might be. He poked his head in through the window and after we explained our dilemma he replied, "Ladies, why don't you try turning on the ignition?" With this advice my friend started the car, hit the automatic window switch and almost decapitated the poor man. I nearly died as I watched the rapidly rising window and the expression on the victim's face that clearly indicated he also thought he might die in the parking lot. Thank you, Lord, for fast reflexes and guardian angels!

❁❁❁❁

Heading across the Anacostia Bridge in Washington, D.C., my friend Lou and I were conversing in the front seat when we became aware of squealing tires behind us. Looking out the rearview mirror we could not help but notice that the traffic had distanced itself from us. In addition we noticed another car whose driver was desperately trying to stay on the bridge as we were seemingly attempting to drive her off of it.

The kids in the back seat told us they were praying big time because they were watching two ladies in the front seat who needed eye contact and hand gestures in order to communicate with one another. Save the world Lord from drivers "out to lunch!"

❁❁❁❁

Getting into my car after 6:30 A.M. mass, I asked my friend if she would direct us out of Norfolk toward our destination which happened to be Pensacola, Florida. She gave me a blank look and responded, "I don't know how." I exclaimed, "What do you mean you don't know how, you've only been there eight times!" "I don't know how," she repeated. We became hysterical. Both of us could see ourselves sitting in St. Gregory's parking lot indefinitely. Miraculously, I happened to have a map of Virginia with me. Normally I do not, therefore, we were able to find our way out of Norfolk and head south. The blind leading the blind.

A priest once told me, "If you know a nutty God, you're holy." It certainly takes one to know one and my friend is a very holy lady.

People do the Strangest Things

Emergencies come and emergencies go. When my husband was in the Air Force he definitely "went" if an emergency occurred. After a tidal wave alert was posted in Hawaii, he naturally vanished in his plane and the only course of action that seemed appropriate for me to take was to go around my house putting up all the curtains so they wouldn't get wet.

Living in Maryland during the Cuban Missile Crisis, the threat of a bomb falling in the area was very real. Once again I was an "abandoned" wife. My friend Lou was busy purchasing sleeping bags and the like to prepare her basement for the worst. I cleaned my attic. I had to do something and my open basement didn't qualify for protection from any fallout.

My husband was flying the owner/manager of Secretariat, the Triple Crown winner, from New York to Boston for the final leg of the derby. Having been invited to join our husbands, Speight's co-pilot's wife and I were asked if we would act as stewardesses for the trip, a role we reluctantly accepted. The crew member who normally did this job had been given the weekend off, so we felt there wasn't any alternative but to perform as best we could.

As the plane left the runway there was a terrible crash when unsecured liquor bottles flew up the aisle. Every hostess knows that all items must be fastened down before takeoff—almost all, that is. Thank goodness they didn't break as they smashed into one another and fortunately they flew low and not high or else there might have been more than a horse race to get excited about that Sunday afternoon. Undoubtedly there was an impression made on the passengers, but not a lasting physical one, Thank you Lord!

Creative Living

When I was busy converting the interior of my house in Maryland from a nice neighborhood creation into the rustic interior which I'd always desired, I decided to begin in the bedroom. My friend Marge and I had found a junk shop in Southern Maryland which sold us an astronomical amount of goodies cheap. We came home with a station wagon loaded with huge eight feet tall old shutters, great picture frames, etc. The shutters I used behind my bed as a headboard but the chests in the room needed some attention. At this time my husband was flying with an old bachelor and when he told him that he had come home to find his chest of drawers pushed into the closet, the man was a little put off. The next time he saw him the gentleman wanted to know what had happened to his chest. Speight replied, "It is now in the basement being beaten with chains for a distressed finish." We might add that this man was now a more confirmed bachelor than ever. My thing was that people, particularly in the service, always talked about what they were going to do when they retired. I decided I would do what I wanted while we were on active duty.

We took an old maraschino cherry barrel and made it into a cradle for our expected child, Richard. Speight used some of the removed staves as rockers. Placed by the side of my bed, it proved to be a wonderful answer for a restless newborn in the middle of the night. This creation wasn't used for long as a crib because Dick was a very active child who was pulling himself up to the coffee table by the age of four months. Later one of my daughter's utilized it as a magazine holder in her living room. Different strokes for different folks.

❀❀❀❀

Sometimes you find amazing things in the woods compliments of God. We desperately needed a double bed for our newly purchased cottage in New Hampshire when one of my kids said, "There's a rusty old iron piece of junk in the woods outback." In the midst of a tumbledown shack stood a wonderful creation just waiting for a coat of paint to make it into a real treasure. Money was a bit of a problem at that time in our lives; therefore, we were ecstatic when a mattress and box spring were found later at a local tag sale. What a wonderful inexpensive gift from the Almighty!

What Is It?

At Mary Lou's home wedding reception my brother-in-law approached my husband and asked why we had an old weathered clutchplate hanging on our living room wall. It happened to be a real treasure that I had discovered laying beside the road on one of my frequent jaunts near our home in Maryland. Reminding me of an Inca calendar, I had placed it amongst the other interesting objects on the barn siding which lined the wall. It took a mechanically inclined plumber to recognize the original purpose for which my prize was assigned. You can fool some of the people some of the time, but not all of the people all of the time. To my knowledge only one other person had ever recognized my "Inca calendar" as being a clutchplate.

Entering our rustic bathroom one was greeted by most unusual towel hangers—old meat hooks, or were they grappling hooks used to pull bodies from their watery graves? Junk yards are full of interesting stuff. Who knows?

One sunny afternoon I decided it was time to finish a decorating project that I had started in our twin daughters' bedroom. After removing some of the weathered split rail fencing from the yard, I proceeded to install it behind the twin beds that lined the wall. This produced wonderful esthetic results—the perfect accompaniment to barn boards and creative rustic shelving.

I was hammering away enthusiastically when I was interrupted by a neighbor who wanted to observe what we were doing to transform our new home into an old creation. At that particular moment I happened to be pounding nails, eighteen of them to be exact, into my living room wall. She was horrified at the sight. Nail holes in walls were an absolute taboo to this lady. In order to hang the old wooden cookie molds that I had purchased, this "abomination" was necessary. Jesus was crucified for love of us, why not that living room wall which would provide me with endless joy?

My husband readily identifies with the lady's reaction. He dies a thousand deaths every time he hears the sound of hammering in our house. Sometimes things do fall off the wall. Enter at your own risk!

❀❀❀❀

My son, Richard, had a very interesting experience at the age of three. One morning I received a phone call from a frantic White House switchboard operator asking me to please remove my son from their "hotline." Dick had discovered the phone that had been hidden in what I considered a safe place. His father, Speight, was pilot and Air Force aide to Vice President Humphrey at the time and, hence, we had several such lines in our home. If you wanted to connect with Tokyo, Moscow, or other various places in the world for official business, all you had to do was make your request known. How many folks do you know who talked to the White House at the age of three?

❀❀❀❀

Dick and I were attending mass early one morning in a church which was located next to the Fire Station. When the bell for the consecration rang, the siren next door went off at the exact same moment. Immediately Dick stood up in the midst of the congregation and yelled out in a loud clear voice, "What's going on around here?"

Strange Answers in Strange Places

Being in the Medjugorje, Yugoslavia area in October was not a warm experience, particularly at night. On my first trip in 1985 we stayed in a house in a neighboring town which was newly constructed, but not well insulated. While laying in bed I could see light shining through cracks in the molding of the balcony door. The nights were bone-chilling and there was no heat, so after trying unsuccessfully to fall asleep for a long period of time I had to find something warm to cover myself with other than the two thin blankets which had been provided. There on the floor was the perfect answer, a large, thick area rug!

The next morning when the landlady appeared, she seemed somewhat flabbergasted to see the displaced piece of carpeting covering her guest's bed. Needless to say, I was given adequate protection from the cold for the rest of my stay.

When my daughter and I were together in Medjugorje for Thanksgiving, the weather was there again bitter cold in the evenings. Even though a small space heater had been provided, my ears froze until I decided to use a pair of underpants as the perfect head covering. Carol took a picture of her mom tucked into bed featuring pink bloomers as a most striking fashion statement. God does provide. You just have to be prepared to look in strange places!

A Heart in the Right Place at the Wrong Time

Cleaning out a shed at my daughter's house in Louisiana, I removed a heavy unmarked box from the shelf and discovered a hornets nest safely tucked in amongst the contents. As they swarmed forth, I frantically heaved the container into the yard. The sound of shattering glass resounded in my ears.

Dishes do come and dishes do go, but I felt pretty awful about the demise of grandmother's heirlooms!

✿✿✿✿

It was an eventful day to say the least, particularly since straightening the carport was my next project. Moving the unusually heavy basketball hoop without any assistance proved to be a disaster. When I yelled for Carol to come quickly, she appeared almost immediately–an unexpected blessing. Together we were able to remove the flying object from the hood and top of her vehicle- not a pretty sight to behold.

Good intentions brought me lots of attention, not much fan mail. You certainly allowed me to come up with soup on my face that day, Lord. No wonder my husband says I should come with a warning label.

✿✿✿✿

Wandering down the street one afternoon I discovered my neighbor ambitiously painting his house. While chatting with him as he worked, I noticed he was having some difficulty moving a heavy ladder, therefore, I generously offered my assistance. As I grappled with the awkward gadget, it slipped out of my hands and crashed through a window located only a few feet away.

My friend clearly expressed that he was not pleased at the thought of having to replace shattered panes of glass in the midst of his project. How could you have allowed such a thing to happen to such a nice man? Lord, so much for good intentions!

Driving Can Be Hazardous

Driving on a back street through a small town in Connecticut I was stopped by a traffic cop who reminded me that I was going thirty-eight miles per hour in a thirty-mile-per-hour zone. He asked to see my driver's license and when I handed him my card he responded, "Lady, this is your MasterCard." I replied, "Well, you know I'm so used to giving it out. Sorry!" He had pulled over a young male on a motorcycle shortly before I arrived on the scene, therefore, he vanished briefly while he took care of his previous commitment.

Returning to my car, he announced he was only giving me a warning and stated, "Please, don't go home and tell your husband about this, because it's just too embarrassing!" Have you ever had such an encounter with a traffic cop?

My grandchildren and I were on our way to play miniature golf in a neighboring Louisiana town. Driving through a small village I suddenly was aware of flashing lights in my rearview mirror as well as the sound of a police siren. Aretha Franklin was performing on the radio and I was busy listening to one of my favorite songs. When the cop approached me I explained to him that I was momentarily "out to lunch" absorbed in the music and unfortunately not my driving. He gave me a blank stare and told me he was giving me a citation whereby I would have to appear in court the following week. However this was not possible

because I was leaving for Connecticut before the date mentioned. The kids in the back of the van were absolutely
silent as all of this took place and the cop kept glancing
back at all of their stricken faces. Finally he announced,
"Go lady, but when you come back through here, you'd
better be observing the speed limit." Returning later we
watched a busy cop writing out a traffic ticket. I wonder if
they had been listening to Aretha Franklin?

❀❀❀❀

Our neighbor and good friend had purchased a used
white Rolls Royce for her husband's Christmas gift. He
wasn't overjoyed with the present and my remark to him
was, "You're the first person I ever met who had to drive
their cross instead of carry it!" My husband's statement to
my yuppie friend was, "It looks just like something Wilt
Chamberlain would drive."

Our first trip in the Rolls Royce was to a dinner in a
neighboring town. Returning home in the back seat of the
vehicle with my husband I had to insist the driver of the car
stop immediately so that I might get out to relieve myself of
the fine meal which I had just consumed.

Have you ever had to throw up while driving in the backseat of a Rolls Royce?

Things Kids Say

I once had a dream that either a child or a grandchild of mine could talk at a very early age. My dream came true when my granddaughter Erica arrived on the scene. Speaking in sentences before the age of one, she had people quite puzzled by her verbal ability. Her mom told me that before Erica was two people would sometimes stop and ask if she were a midget.

When Erica was eighteen months old her mom was trying desperately to get her to take medicine for an ear infection in the wee hours of the morning. Resisting with all her might, she finally said to her mom, "I hear the phone ringing Mom and you had better answer it!"

❀❀❀❀

Flying from New York to Oklahoma I happened to be sitting next to a very nice lady who also had twins in her life. We were able to share many of our experiences in raising "two for the price of one." I had a cartoon at home on my fridge door showing a young boy with hands on his hips exclaiming to his mom and dad who were at the front doorway holding triplets in their arms, "You had better get on the phone right now because you're going to have a tougher time getting rid of those than the kittens." She also had the same cartoon on her bulletin board and it was at least fifteen years old, but ageless.

While I danced around my daughter's living room my four-year-old granddaughter Elaine remarked to her father, "Why don't you ask her to marry you, dad?"

Treasure Inside or Out?

The phone call from a friend came late one cold, winter afternoon. The local A & P grocery store was redoing their meat department and they had thrown some wonderful old meat hooks in the garbage area behind the store. I immediately got in touch with another friend Eugenia, and off we headed with four-year-old Sarah and her friend Denise in the back seat of our Volkswagen bug. Needless to say, we had high hopes of multiple treasures in our heads. Too bad the meat hooks were no longer there, but outside of an upholstery shop was an old discarded sofa with wonderful down cushions. The two kids in the backseat ended up riding comfortably close to the bug's ceiling that night! (Those were the days without seat belt regulations.)

After scouting the area thoroughly, we headed for a small group of stores that were all closed, however, we did notice a light on in an office located upstairs in the large building. As we drove around back in search of goodies, our car engine suddenly died and refused to start. At 6:30 on a cold winter night with two little ones in tow, we were not overjoyed with the situation. A telephone had to be found so we climbed the steps to the lighted office above in high hopes of success. On the door was a plaque announcing a psychiatrist dwelt therein. You would have loved the look of glee on the doctor's face as we explained our situation and he beheld Eugenia in her mink coat, high heels, made up to perfection with me in my dungarees, old jacket and messy appearance. (I always did say God put me on this earth to make other people look good.) When I phoned Eugenia to go junking, she had just returned from an afternoon outing, therefore, she did not change clothes but jumped into the car "as is."

Never mind the goodies in the trash bin outside, this guy knew he had his treasure standing right before him in his office. We made our phone call, but unfortunately no appointment with "our friend."

Seeing Red

My neighbor, Ellen, borrowed my red Datsun sedan one afternoon since hers was at the garage being repaired. After she returned the vehicle to my driveway she phoned me from home and related this wild adventure.

Ellen parked the car in front of the store she needed to visit, returned after her errand, retrieved the keys from above the visor where she had placed them and departed for home. In the meantime she noticed the gas tank was almost empty, therefore as a kind gesture Ellen decided to stop at the filling station around the corner. While the attendant was busy filling the car, she became aware that her knapsack, which she had put in the backseat was missing. A magazine was still on the front seat and a tiny hole was in the right-hand side of the windshield. These things Ellen had noticed in my car when she drove away from the house, but looking in the back again she realized this was a red station wagon not a sedan. It went back a lot farther than my auto. Ellen mentioned to the man, who was putting gas in the tank, she had taken someone else's car and needed to return it immediately. In the meantime, Ellen observed a young male on a bicycle directly across the street who was gazing at her intently. A police siren sounded as she left the station, which made Ellen a nervous wreck until she replaced the vehicle with the keys above the visor where she had found them and headed for home.

After she arrived at her house, the phone rang. A woman's voice announced she was the police calling about a stolen vehicle. Ellen was horrified until the lady burst out laughing and announced she was the owner of the car Ellen had taken. This woman's son had called her at work to tell her some strange lady was at the service station getting gas in her car. When she went outside to check if her auto was missing, it was parked where she had left it, consequently she called her son a liar. As she left work later, the lady became aware that her almost empty gas tank was now full, so she decided to check with the gas attendant at the station, who identified Ellen and provided the woman with her name—hence the phone call. Moral of this story is- lock your car and don't leave the keys above the visor or you may have an Ellen in your life!

Keys Will Be Keys

As we scouted the New Hampshire countryside for desirable property, my friend suddenly decided she needed to find a restroom, pronto. After we located a small store with a gas station attached, she adjourned to the potty and I chose to remain in the car. Time passed—15 minutes, 20 minutes. Where on earth did this woman go? I did not feel called to go inside but waited patiently until she emerged. Her problem was the car keys had vanished somewhere within the shop. She had double-checked the bathroom as well as other areas where she had picked up a few items. Nowhere were the keys to be found. They were visiting from Virginia in a newly purchased vehicle, therefore, I did inquire if her husband had an extra set of keys which she said he did. It then occurred to me she needed to go check her underpants in the toilet, since that was the last place she definitely saw them. When she emerged again only a few minutes later with keys in her hand, I asked her if she told the clerk at the checkout counter where she had located them. She replied, "No, I only said I found them." Whereby I retorted, "Why didn't you tell him you were sitting on them? It would have made his day!" Too bad the man in the store had to miss out on all the laughs we shared that day.

Where Did You Come From?

As I shopped around in one of the local junk shops, I wondered if the manager's wife appreciated all those wonderful buys as I did. When I paid for my purchases, I inquired if his spouse was as enthusiastic about second-hand shopping as I was. He replied, "No, my wife wasn't raised that way." My mother, who would not have been caught dead in such a place, must have turned over in her grave that day.

✿✿✿✿

My friend's daughter, Lisa, had stopped to visit us during her travels around the country. We had dropped off several of my kids at the local high school early that morning and decided to head for the junk shop in a neighboring town. Both of us were very enamored with good used merchandise at this time in our lives, however, neither one of us had on shopping apparel at the moment. I was barefoot and in my nightgown, but it was a short flowered creation, so I felt it was passable for this particular expedition. It proved to be an excellent time for bargains and as the lady bagged our finds she inquired, "Are you walking?" The store was located in an extremely poverty ridden area of the city. We undoubtedly looked the part that morning, which definitely is OK, Lord.

✿✿✿✿

Before my total change of allegiance from local furniture store to local junk shop, I went with a friend to purchase a new sofa and chair at a very nice establishment in Washington, D.C. The clerk who waited on us was a pleasant chap, but not someone with an obvious sense of humor. I dashed around the store and grabbed various pillows scattered here and there in order to see what could possibly go colorwise with the blue sofa I was contemplating buying. As this process continued for a rather long period of time, my friend finally remarked to the salesman, "I hope you don't have the right color underpants on this morning, or you're in big trouble!" The stricken look on the gentleman's face was priceless. I know he wondered what planet we came from that morning!

A House Full of Surprises

A young man who was sitting in our house in Connecticut one cold winter evening suddenly became silent in the midst of our conversation. He had a very puzzled look on his face as he asked, "Is that pole moving?" In our living room we had a large upright beam in the middle of the floor that divided the conversation area from the rest of the room. It was not a structure support beam- strictly for ornamental purposes but gave the appearance of holding up an old beam in the ceiling. Not wanting to drive nails into the wooden floor, I had requested my husband to simply attach it from the ceiling and not from below. All the old wood in our house shrank during the winter months from heat and lack of moisture in the air. Speight had cut the beam and wedged it into place during warm humid weather. Obviously, there was a breeze moving through the living room that night, therefore, he was right, the beam was swaying. I do not believe he ever returned to our house again—most likely believing it was a life-threatening situation.

As I always said, "We managed to separate the men from the boys." He should have been more terrified of the inhabitants in the house than the structure of the house.

❁❁❁❁❁

My daughter Barbara and I attended a sale at a church in Oklahoma that was selling all of their old church pews, amongst other things. When we returned home with our new found goody, we immediately decided to clean up the item for future refinishing. When we turned over this heavy eight-foot bench, we beheld the most amazing array of what seemed to be varied shades of fungi growing beneath the seat. Upon closer inspection, we discovered this to be hundreds of pieces of multi-colored chewing gum—forty or fifty years worth at least. Now we know for sure where people dispose of their gum while in church. Could one of those pieces have been yours?

Answering a knock on my door late one afternoon, I was greeted by my son's friend Dean, who when he entered our house, was surprised by a white sheet partially covering the Indian rug in the hall. In response to Dean's quizzical look and his question, "What's that?" I removed the material from the now deceased body of Winnie, our German Shepherd who had expired in the middle of the night. Dean was taken aback by the exposure, but since a large dead animal was too heavy for me to remove by myself, I was awaiting assistance from some members of my family. Winnie had been ill for several months, therefore, it was not a surprise but very much a blessing that she died peacefully by herself without assistance. Winnie had good taste. She was a beautiful body resting on a beautiful rug!

Ain't Seen Nothing Yet

Father was busy baptizing the RCIA group at St. Maria Goretti Church in Scottsdale on Holy Saturday evening. We gathered outside by the fountain after mass and observed the priest who performing each ceremony would exclaim to the newly baptized, "You ain't seen nothing yet!" This happened to be my birthday and after the service I approached Father to say, "You ain't seen nothing yet, is my birthday present from God tonight, Father."

Believe me, that was seven years ago and in retrospect I know I hadn't seen anything yet. I can guarantee, that all those folks who were baptized that night had not seen anything yet either. Life is unbelievable with God if you're seriously trying to do His Will. God is a blast and hopefully, He will blast you right into heaven someday. Not any of us have seen anything yet!

Age—More or Less

One thing I've learned is not to ask people how old they think I am when they inquire about my age. On a pilgrimage one Easter a lady with whom my roommate and I were discussing age looked much younger than she was. She never actually disclosed her age but responded to this fact by adjusting her children's ages to correspond to what we perceived her age to be. It was bizarre to watch her mentally knock off years from how old they were as she discussed their accomplishments. Stupidly, I set myself up by asking how old she thought I was. When she responded seventy and I was only sixty-five, vanity of vanities, it bothered me until the next day when a gentleman in our group asked me my age and when I told him, he exclaimed, "I thought you were much younger than that!" God does have a sense of humor!

Have you ever noticed when you look in the mirror some mornings and think, "Gee, I look pretty good today," someone invariably comes up to inquire, "Have you been ill?" The opposite has happened when I think I look awful and a person remarks, "Golly, you're looking great! Have you lost weight?" I have a friend who never fails to ask me if I've lost weight every time I gain a few pounds or more. Is God trying to tell us something? How you perceive your physical being momentarily can be rather nonsense? Don't take yourself too seriously.

When I mentioned to Speight that someone thought I was younger than my age, my husband retorted, "Nobody ever met anyone as old as you who acts the way you do." He also told a bible study group his wife should come with a warning label. Watch out for old explosives! They can be dangerous, right God?

My forty-five year old daughter's friend told her she was getting old. She exclaimed, "No, I'm going to be just like my mom, immature." Hopefully she means childlike and not childish.

Andrew, my friend Andy's son ,used to think of me as his contemporary. We had a very special spiritual hookup from the time he was born. One day as we played games together, I felt what was being asked of me was out of my fifty-year-old league and remarked to Andrew that I was simply getting too old to participate in what he wished me to do. He was horrified at the thought. I repeated my feelings to him once more and after mulling this over for a short period of time, he exclaimed, "Drummy (his name for me) you're not getting old, you're getting new!" These exact words of wisdom from the mouth of a three year old, I have repeated time and time again to those who say to me, "I'm getting old!" Each day we are a new creation, particularly if we are willing to say "Yes" to God. There is a whole new world to be experienced every twenty-four hours, if we sincerely desire to relinquish our will for His will.

Love It and Leave It

My friend Andy mentioned to me she was terrified one day while eating at my dining room table. A piece of the decoration fell off into her lap and she was convinced she had wrecked the table. We had not known each other very long at this time hence her apprehension because my answer to decorating was tack it on or tack it up, however, if that didn't work then you had to go for a more permanent approach. The item which fell off the table apparently had been tacked on—no big deal. If at first you don't succeed, try try again.

When Andy, a great junk lover herself, first came to my house in Wilton she told me if she ever died and went to heaven she hoped it would look just like this. Father remarked it looked like the African veld with all the animal skins, while another gal thought it looked as if it belonged out West. Visitors either loved it or felt very threatened by the unusual rustic atmosphere. I had organized collections of old bric-a-brac everywhere. One day I called Andy and announced I had removed my numerous brass candlesticks from the dining room table and placed them in the basement. She remarked, "If you had told me you had gone down on Route 7 and thrown yourself in front of a passing car, I would have found it more believable."

I did tell a friend once they might read headlines in the newspaper one day stating, "Murder at a local tag sale!" Andy and I liked similar stuff and would often dash for the same item at the same time. There were a few tense moments.

❀❀❀❀

I dreamed one night someone came and stole my old copper pans. I was amazed to find when I awakened I was not traumatized by the loss. God was extricating me from my possessions. The next step for me was to actually get rid of them. A week before my son Chris' wedding we had a giant tag sale and sold three quarters of the stuff in our house. Junkies thought they had died and gone to heaven. Many came two days in a row. I could not have traveled in years to come if my attachment to things had not been severed. Too many intriguing collectibles exist in other countries for me to have been able to resist their lure if I were still relishing the old, the different, the interesting rather than the ultimate—God. God had to be the biggie in my life, not old stuff!

Wild Tales

One afternoon there was great activity in the meadow by the front porch of our house. I saw Ima, our black cat, chasing a cardinal, whom she had obviously caught and let go momentarily, into the long meadow grass in front of my kitchen window. Dashing out of the house after the wayward animal, I approached a very determined cat attempting to subdue an equally feisty red bird. It had never occurred to me that cardinals could be as aggressive as this bird was towards her captor. There was a fierce battle going on before I was able to grab Ima and enclose her in the house. When I returned to the meadow, I found a badly ruffled cardinal, who was able to fly into a nearby bush, seemingly in good shape despite his ordeal.

After Mass the next morning I beheld one beautiful red feather on my door stoop. Since there were no other feathers visible in the yard, this had to be Mr. Cardinal's special "thank you" to his deliverer. At this time of my life bird feathers were included among my collectibles.

My husband and I were driving one afternoon in New Hampshire when we noticed, in the middle of a meadow, a large red fox who was poised ready to pounce on his prey. We turned around quickly and returned to watch the action. However, when the fox saw us sitting in the car observing him, he decided to sit down and gaze at us. After staring for at least five minutes he lost interest in both his meadow find and the strange characters on the road, and wandered off into the nearby woods.

❀❀❀❀

My daughter Sarah and I were busy visiting the animals at the Phoenix Zoo. It was an unusually warm Sunday afternoon and very few visitors were present. As we passed the lion enclosure, a huge male was intent on observing something in a rocky formation close by. Finally he assumed his stalking position, crouching with his rear wiggling he pounced and came forth with a huge rat in his mouth. Unfortunately, when this beast landed on the small critter, it was the demise of what he hoped to be a diversion for the afternoon. No amount of coaxing with his paw or mouth could bring forth any sign of life from the rat and he was devastated. Finally, he went over to a tree, sat down and roared. Things obviously were not going his way that day.

❀❀❀❀

At 2:30 A.M. one morning my husband was busy yelling, "Nancy, would you please stop arguing with the cat and come to bed!" Lincoln, our large black tom cat had awakened me with his loud meowing on the front steps of our house. Opening the door, I was greeted by a pet who had a mouse in his mouth. However, every time he yelled for me to open the door, he had to drop it and then quickly catch it once more. We were at a stalemate. I demanded he drop the mouse before I would allow him in the door and he was just as determined to bring the small creature in the house. Eventually he did let go long enough for me to believe it was safe to open the door, however, I was mistaken. He grabbed the animal in his mouth, dashed in the door, ran into the kitchen and dropped the lively mouse in his dish. Almost immediately the mouse vanished under the baseboard heating vents in the hall and Lincoln giving it his best try could not find his treasure. Climbing back into bed I gave it my best try to fall asleep with a new found friend somewhere nearby.

❀❀❀❀

Early one morning I was swimming by the dam on our lake in New Hampshire when a quarter of a mile out from shore a loon appeared by my side. We gazed at each other intently until suddenly he disappeared and swimming underneath me he appeared on the other side. Once more we observed each other until eventually he lost interest and swam away to the opposite side of the lake. While he was submerged beneath me I could only think of his long sharp bill. Thank goodness he did not choose to examine the intruder more closely or to taste the merchandise.

The End of the Tale

When we first moved to Connecticut, we were in great need of furnishings for a house which was at least twice as big as our former dwelling. Since we had six kids with the seventh on the way, we had no choice but to seek secondhand merchandise. Tag sales, junk shops, and dumps were our happy hunting grounds. My daughter, Nancy, once remarked garage sales were not simply junk buying sprees for me, but social events as well. It was great fun to talk with the sellers and even get a tour of their homes.

One Saturday we were blessed by being able to find two wonderful chests–cheap. Our means of transportation that morning was a Volkswagen bug, therefore it was necessary for us to return home to pick up the station wagon in order to transport our treasure. When we returned, the debonair old gentleman in his Greek sea captain's hat, who had sold us the chests, was completely traumatized by what had occurred during our absence. While we were gone, two men came who wished to buy one of the old bureaus, but they were informed this was not possible since it had already been bought and paid for. They hassled with him unrelentlessly until one of them made a disgusting remark then turned around and dropped his pants in the old man's face.

A friend of mines comment to this story was, "What a wild tale!" or perhaps tail?

Eugenia and I had just dropped my husband off at Westchester County Airport and were driving back to

Connecticut through Bedford, New York when we spied a garage sale sign that we could not resist. It was early Sunday morning and any real junkie knows the early bird gets the goodies.

As we approached the front doors after driving up a long winding driveway I stopped at the wing on the left and Eugenia proceeded around to the addition on the right. A door was ajar and I entered a room where all sorts of clutter was tossed around on the floor. It was a disaster area, but no one was in sight for the sale, so I decided to knock on the front door. Eugenia in the meantime joined me exclaiming what wonderful athletic equipment was to be found in the other end of the house.

There was no response to my banging and I noticed a bedroom window on the second floor was open. If someone were still in bed, they had to have heard our discussion about the big mess in one end of the house as well as the lovely sporting goods in the other end and no way could they possibly have been unaware of my loud knocking. It suddenly occurred to us, they were not having a garage sale. The sign must have been indicative of one being conducted down the road. We became hysterical thinking about our boo-boo as we hastened to our car. Just as we were about to leave the driveway, a vehicle roared up and a male occupant demanded to know what we were doing there. This no doubt was a neighbor who had been called by someone with an absentee husband. We explained how sorry we were to have caused such a problem and departed—the two would-be burglars casing the joint early one Sunday morning.

Epilogue

After receiving communion during Sunday Mass, it occurred to me to ask God why he wanted a book written about His sense of humor. His response to me was that most people think of Him as a terrorist, not as a lover and certainly not as a humorist.

The explanation for terrorist seems to be "fear of God." Fear of dying to self. Fear of being out of control and God being in control. Since we all wish to be God, this is terror. If God couldn't laugh at our antics, he would have wiped us all off the face of the earth a long time ago.

How could he possibly have lived with those Twelve Apostles for three years, a motley crew, and not have laughed at their bloopers and blunders. Appreciation for His sense of humor is the name of the game. Relax, and let God enjoy you for a while.